OFFICE
OF THE
PROPHET
A COMPREHENSIVE STUDY

JANICE E. WAGNER

CITI OF
BOOKS

CITIOFBOOKS, INC.
3736 Eubank NE Suite A1
Albuquerque, NM 87111-3579
www. citiofbooks. com

Hotline: 1 (877) 389-2759
Fax: 1 (505) 930-7244

Ordering Information:
Quantity sales. Special discounts are available on quantity purchases by corporations, associations, and others. For details, contact the publisher at the address above.

Printed in the United States of America.

ISBN-13:	Paperback	979-8-89391-212-8
	Hardback	979-8-89391-214-2
	eBook	979-8-89391-213-5

Library of Congress Control Number: 2024914493

OFFICE OF THE PROPHET
A Comprehensive Study

What is a Prophet of God?

How does Someone Know They are a Prophet?

How Does the Holy Spirit Operate

in the Life of a Prophet?

What are the Responsibilities of a Prophet?

AUTOBIOGRAPHY

I consider myself to be a relatively normal human being. I graduated from Elizabeth Forward High School in Pennsylvania in 1972, and attended Bradford (Business) School graduating with a diploma in Legal Secretarial Studies in 1974.

I received Jesus as my personal Lord and Savior at the age of 12. Throughout my life I have suffered through many trials. Some of those trials have included multiple health challenges. I have been at death's door several times only to be spared by the power of the Lord. I have received healing upon healing in my life (physical, emotional, and spiritual) and the Lord has poured out many miracles as well.

Twice in my life my family has had to sell everything we owned and start over in a new state that we had never even visited before. I was born in Pennsylvania and moved to various locations within that state until God sent our family to Georgia to start a new life. After living in Georgia for 15 years, the Lord moved our family to Santa Fe, New Mexico. Each of these moves had their own challenges.

As a Christian, I have learned not to ask the Lord why; rather my question to Him when trials come into my life is, "Lord how can my experiencing this trial bring honor to your name?" Of course, that question usually comes after a lot of whining, crying and complaining.

I am an ordinary person who loves the Lord with all my heart. I have to be honest with you I have made many mistakes in life. I have sinned in many ways that I do not wish to disclose, the Lord has transformed my Life and I am no longer the person who did those things. I give all glory to the Father, Son, and the Holy Spirit for who I am today, and all that the Lord has done in and through me. Because of the sin in my life, I spent many years bound by guilt and shame. It was through my sin and failures that I learned our Lord isn't hiding behind every tree waiting to smack me in the head. He did not come to this earth to condemn me. He forgives as soon as I repent.

In June of 1979, just before I gave birth to my first son, the Lord spoke to me after a seriously long time of repentance, and He called me to be His mouthpiece to the body of Christ. I was humbled that the Lord would place this call upon me after all the ways I had failed Him. I told Him I thought He was making a big mistake, and when He figured that out, He could take His calling back. Well, He has never taken His calling back, nor has He lifted His anointing from me. In fact, as I have learned to trust Him more and more over the years, His anointing has become stronger, and He has developed boldness within me to speak for Him in powerful ways. It has been a 40 plus year journey of ministering under His anointing and His call.

When I look back over my life of service to the Lord, I am amazed by the ways He has used me and the words He has given to the body of Christ through me. I recognize that it is truly the Lord speaking through me because there is nothing good in me except Him. The things I speak come directly from the Lord. He gets the honor and glory for anything that is accomplished.

If the Lord can use someone like me to minister for Him, I know He can speak through any of His children once they have been infused with the power of the Holy Spirit. The challenge is to take the time to listen for the Lord's voice and simply repeat to the body of Christ what you hear.

If you have received the baptism of the Holy Spirit and He has placed His anointing upon you and commissioned you to minister in the office of a prophet of God, fasten your seat belt. It's going to be an interesting journey.

PREFACE

Before you get into this study, it might be beneficial to tell you a few things about my writing style. I was educated in the 1960's where if a person was referring to both male and female the pronoun used would be the male form and it was inclusive of the female. I am not one who worries about being politically correct. If you get offended by such things, this may be a problem as you get into this study.

Unless otherwise noted in the study my scripture references come from the New International Version of the Bible. I admit that there are some differences between the New International and the King James Version of the Bible. In some cases, I believe that the King James Version has the best interpretation. There are many other translations of the Bible available today. Choose a translation that best ministers to your needs. For me personally, the New International Version is the one I best relate to when reading and studying for myself.

This study came about from a teaching on the manifestation gifts of the Holy Spirit that was prepared for the altar workers at The People's Church of Santa Fe, New Mexico. As I was discussing the gift of prophecy, I stated that anyone who knows Jesus as their Savior, and has the infilling of the Holy Spirit, can prophesy if they know what the Lord wants to say to His people. I also stated that simply operating through the manifestation gift of prophecy did not make someone a prophet.

I discussed the fact that the manifestation gift of prophecy is not for prediction. The scripture texts will be included in the study itself, but basic prophecy is for edification (instruction), exhortation (encouragement), and comfort. I also stated that when prophets prophesy, their words often contain revelation. At this point several people in the class asked what the difference was between the gift of prophecy and the office of the prophet. That was when this study was born.

The Lord used different prophets for many different purposes. There were very powerful prophets, and there were prophets who seemed to have less powerful roles as prophets. Some performed powerful miracles; others have no recorded miracles having been done at their hands.

This study discusses how a believer knows he is a prophet, and how the Lord used various prophets in the Old and New Testaments. The study discusses the differences between the prophets of the Old and New Testaments. It discusses the reason why God sends prophets, and how He has operated through them in the past and in current times.

Studying the Bible is something that everyone should do for themselves. There is also a place for personal testimonies of how the Holy Spirit has operated over the years. Since I am the person doing this study, it seemed appropriate to relate some of the ways the Lord has operated through me as I have served in the office of the prophet over many years. Each believer in the Lord Jesus Christ has a story to tell. Some of those stories are more interesting than others. I felt that including some of the more interesting personal experiences from my life would give the Lord glory. Everything I share from my life is true and accurate to the best of my memory.

The way the Holy Spirit has operated through me is a perfect example of how the Lord places His anointing on very ordinary and imperfect people to accomplish His purposes on the earth. It is my hope that the personal experiences I have related in this study will help you understand that if God can work through someone like me, He can work through anyone who is humble in heart and willing to respond to the Holy Spirit when He speaks. All you have to do is be willing to die to self and let Him take over.

I want to thank God the Father, Jesus Christ the Son, and the Holy Spirit of God for breathing into me this study, and allowing me to put it to paper. I recognize that the things I do myself don't have life in them; it is only when the Holy Spirit anoints a work that life can be contained therein.

As I look at the completed manuscript, I am amazed at the journey the Lord has brought me through. I do not have a college degree; my highest level of schooling is business school. To tell you that I feel inadequate to have put this study together would be a vast understatement. It is a work that the Lord has done through me, and I pray each person going through this study will be taught by the Holy Spirit who is the greatest teacher in the world.

Table of Contents

Chapter	Description	Page
1	Introduction	1
2	Prophet – God's Definition	9
3	Through Whom does the Lord Speak?	18
4	The Baptism of the Holy Spirit	24
5	Responding to the Holy Spirit	33
6	Prerequisites to Serve as a Prophet of God	38
7	The Manifestation Gifts – Tools for the Prophe	42
8	Utterance Gifts	53
9	Revelation Gifts	65
10	Power Gifts	81
11	Church Order, Protocols and Discipline	95
12	Prophets Outside of the Pentecostal Community	103
13	Prophets and the Working of Miracles	108
14	Characteristics of a Prophet	111
15	Suffering	134
16	Distinguishing Between True and False Prophets	142
17	The Call to the Office of a Prophet	149
18	Prayer can Change the Mind of God	155
19	Prophets have Varying Levels of Spiritual Power	158
20	Prophet as the Voice of God	161
21	Prophets – Old Testament Verses New Testament	166
22	God's Prophets can Speak Their Mind to the Lord	179
23	Experienced Prophets Mentor Newer Prophets	184
24	Closing	193

CHAPTER 1

INTRODUCTION

M ost churches in this day and age are ignorant of what the office of the prophet is, and how those anointed to serve in this office operate in the church and in the world at large. There must be someone teaching on this subject, but I have not encountered anyone. It is imperative for the people of God be able to recognize these individuals because the office of the prophet was established by God Himself. It is God who anoints and appoints prophets to be His voice to the body of Christ and to the nations.

Scripture says of prophets: "Surely the Sovereign Lord does nothing without revealing His plan to His servants the prophets." (Amos 3:7) Notice this scripture refers to His prophets as servants. They are servants of the Lord in word and deed.

When the Lord gives revelation through His prophets, God will validate what the prophet speaks. Throughout scripture you will find phrases that include: "Fulfilling the word the Lord had spoken through His prophet." (I Kings 2:27); "According to the word of the Lord" (II Kings 1:17); and "But this is how God fulfilled what He had foretold through all the prophets." (Acts 3:18) These scriptures indicate the Lord will bring to pass messages spoken by His prophets under the direction of God.

Jesus said, "Whoever welcomes a prophet as a prophet, will receive a prophet's reward." (Matthew 10:41)

These scriptures make it quite apparent that the Lord values His prophets.

I want to thank Pastor Bob Baca for asking me to put this teaching together. I have never had the benefit of participating in a teaching on the office of the prophet. What I know has come from the Holy Spirit as He has taught me how to operate in this office over the years.

In studying and compiling this teaching, the Holy Spirit reaffirmed His call upon me to minister in this office. I do not say this lightly, or to make anyone feel that I am more favored by God than others. It is a humbling and awesome responsibility that requires great diligence to be sure I am hearing the Lord and following what He is directing me to do and say.

Through studying the office of the prophet, I discovered that many of the things I have done over the years and the ways the Lord has had me minister are all part of the office of the prophet. I was doing what the Lord told me to do, and I was ministering in the way the Lord called me to minister, but I was unfamiliar with the characteristics that set me apart to minister in this office. I learned a great deal through preparing this teaching, and I pray that each person studying it will learn as well. Of course, the Holy Spirit is the perfect teacher, and I invite Him to open your minds and hearts to hear His voice as you go through this study.

Let's start with the basics. Many people in the body of Christ today believe that the Old Testament became outdated when the Lord sent His son Jesus Christ into the world to be our Lord and Redeemer. In fact, many people do not even read the Old Testament due to this kind of thinking.

The Old Testament sets forth the history of the church itself, which is fundamental for believers. It introduces the statutes the Lord set forth for His people to follow; this is also beneficial for the body of Christ. The Old Testament establishes a moral code authored by God Himself. The Old Testament is also filled with example after example of how the Lord worked through His anointed prophets.

The Old Testament also contains demonstrations of the Lord, through His prophets, instructing the people of Israel, correcting them, and revealing what was going to happen in the future. The Old Testament includes demonstrations of God's wrath being poured out against those who disobeyed God. There is much to be learned from studying the Old Testament. There are also outdated laws like an eye for an eye and a tooth for a tooth, that are no longer followed. We are living in an age of grace and mercy that requires us to forgive instead of imparting retribution.

One of my teaching techniques is to include true stories about my own personal life experiences. I find that this can make the teaching more relatable. As you read this information, if something strikes a chord with you, please take note and apply it. If a point is important, it may be repeated more than once throughout the book. Repetition is another one of my teaching techniques. You may disagree with some of what I say, and you may actually take offense at times. Please pray about these points and ask the Lord for clarity.

This book is designed to take away some of the mystery surrounding the Holy Spirit and His manifestation gifts. We will discuss each of these gifts. We will discuss how the Holy Spirit has operated these gifts in and through me for more than 40 years. There are several ways people refer to the gifts of the Holy Spirit. They can be called manifestation gifts, workings, affirmations, enablement's, or even empowerments of the Holy Spirit. I will refer to them as they are referred to in I Corinthians 12:7, "Now to each one is given the manifestation of the Spirit for the common good."

The baptism of the Holy Spirit, and the gifts He brings with Him when we receive His infilling, operate in power and strength in the church and in each individual believer. Even when a Spirit-filled believer does not operate publicly, the Holy Spirit will often activate His gifts in our private lives as we witness to others. The Spirit Himself encourages the believer to live uninfluenced by the world. As we learn to rely on Him, the believer grows in the things of the Spirit and in the character of God. The Holy Spirit imparts power in the believer to be continually transformed into the image of God.

The more we allow His transforming work to continue in our lives, the more our love for God will grow, and the more our love for others will become evident. The Spirit encourages us to be pure in heart and have a good conscience. As we are transformed, we will develop a sincere faith in God the Father, Jesus His Son, and the Holy Spirit. The Holy Spirit gives us power to live as Jesus lived.

When the baptism of the Holy Spirit is received, we are infused with power from on high. He comes bringing gifts for those who will receive Him. The manifestation gifts have both a public and private operation. Because people are often unaware of how these gifts can operate privately, they sometimes ignore or overlook their operation. The private operation of these gifts can be even more effective and powerful than the public operation. For instance, the gift of speaking in tongues can be a powerful tool for intercession. Few people will ever yield to the Spirit to speak a message in tongues in a church service, but perhaps the more important function of the gift of speaking in tongues is when we use this gift while we are interceding, as the Lord calls all believers to do.

One of the greatest benefits to the private operation of the manifestation gifts is the spiritual strength that is built, and the closeness that develops between the Holy Spirit and a believer as they learn to allow Him to operate in and through them.

One could spend many hours studying these gifts, I have several Bible commentaries; each of them treats these gifts differently. Some just gloss over the baptism of the Holy Spirit and the manifestation gifts associated with Him.

If you recall, when God started talking with Samuel in I Samuel 3, he thought Eli, the High Priest, was calling him. Samuel went running to him three times before Eli realized it was the voice of God Samuel was hearing. He then taught Samuel how to respond when God spoke. As we each begin to recognize the voice of the Holy Spirit speaking to us, and we respond to His voice, it will then be possible for Him to use us as His hand extended to others.

Understand that operating through the gifts of the Holy Spirit is not restricted to prophets of God. He can and will use anyone who has been born again, and has been baptized in the Holy Spirit. That is when the manifestation gifts of the Holy Spirit become available to the believer. The believer must be willing to yield to the Spirit.

There are many churches in the world today. There are many different denominations as well. Each church has their own teaching about the Holy Spirit and His manifestation gifts. Many ignore these gifts completely. Some just breeze past the chapters of the Bible that talk about these gifts. Some teach that these gifts are no longer in operation today. This is very sad to me, because I know that the Holy Spirit ministers in and through me, and many other believers.

When someone ministers through one of the manifestation gifts, it is not because that person has more of God's favor than others, and it doesn't make them special. The Holy Spirit will speak through anyone willing to yield to Him.

If you have a friend that you like to spend time with, and you take the time to get to know that friend, you will grow very close. That friend may share their problems or perhaps talk about the hard times they have gone through in their life. You may tell that friend the trials you are going through, and the ones you have conquered in your own life. That is how I describe my relationship with the Lord. No one on this earth knows me better than my Lord and Savior. I talk to Him about all that is on my heart and mind, I discuss the trials I am going through, I discuss the things that have hurt me deeply throughout my life, I ask for His wisdom in dealing with my problems; then, I give Him time to speak to me.

I have to say He is my closest and most trusted friend. He can be trusted with anything I am battling in My life, and He will never betray my trust. This is the relationship He wants to have with each one of us. He will be that close friend to anyone willing spend time pursuing Him.

This teaching will not cover all aspects of the baptism of the Holy Spirit and the manifestation gifts. It will be comprehensive, but I am sure there are things I will not touch on.

Before we get into the actual study on the Holy Spirit and His gifts, I think it is expedient to discuss the most important aspects of any type of ministry we do for the Lord. Everything we do should be done as an offering to Him. This is true even if the service we are performing is cleaning toilets at our local church. The thing is, the attitude with which we serve is as important as our service. If we serve Him joyfully, our sacrifice will be received as sweet smelling to Him. Serving to impress people, or out of obligation while complaining, will not be as pleasing to Him. This is because our motivation is incorrect. When we do ministry under the anointing of the Holy Spirit, it must be done in love!

I Corinthians 13:1-2 reads, "If I speak in the tongues of men and of angels, but have not love, I am only a resounding gong or a clanging cymbal. If I have the gift of prophecy and can fathom all mysteries and all knowledge, and if I have absolute faith so as to move mountains, but have not love, I am nothing."

The entire chapter of I Corinthians 13 makes it very clear that God encourages us to have a godly character. More than any ministry we do, more than the faith through which we operate, more than any manifestation gifts that the Holy Spirit may operate through us, God values His character in us, and the love with which we minister. In fact, all the fruit of the Spirit is important when it comes to ministering in any way for the Lord. The greatest in the kingdom of God will be the one who most closely resembles and demonstrates genuine love for God and for every person to whom they minister. I Corinthians 13:13 reads, "And now these three remain, faith, hope and love. But the greatest of these is love."

God does not choose people to minister through the manifestation gifts because they are perfect, or because they have "arrived" at a spiritual maturity level that puts them above others. He works through them because He sees a willing vessel. Some of the vessels through which He chooses to minister are dented, bruised, tarnished, blemished, scratched, some have been cracked, and some have been shattered. What I mean is they have been through testing in their own lives and survived. There are many lessons to be learned through trials. Maturity comes as we learn to walk hand-in-hand with Jesus while the fire rages around us. We should never minister in judgment; we must minister with great compassion, caring, and in love. Even if the Holy Spirit is speaking correction to someone, it must be done in love.

Questions for Study and Discussion

1. Who created the office of the prophet?

2. According to Amos 3:7 what are prophets?

3. Is the Old Testament outdated or is it relevant to our walk with Christ today?

4. Discuss some of the benefits that we gain from reading and studying the Old Testament.

5. What is more important to God than the service we perform for Him?

6. No matter what ministry we perform for the Lord, we must minister in what?

7. Name several ways people refer to the manifestation gifts of the Holy Spirit.

8. When the Holy Spirit is imparted, what does He bring with Him as He comes to dwell within the believer?

9. What qualifies someone to minister through the manifestation of the Holy Spirit?

10. What is the most important part of any service we do for to the Lord?

CHAPTER 2

PROPHET - GOD'S DEFINITION

People often declare someone to be a prophet of God because of the operation of the gift of prophecy in their lives. The manifestation of the gift of prophecy is different from the office of a prophet. Any Spirit-filled believer who knows what the Lord wants to say can speak that message to the body of Christ. A Spirit-filled believer can operate through the gift of prophecy often and for many years but still not be a prophet of God.

One of the big questions people ask about prophets is how does someone know that they are actually called to be a prophet of God? The answer is simple and yet complicated. A prophet will know that he is a prophet when the Lord speaks to him and places a holy call or commission upon him to be a spokesman or messenger for the Lord. This commission can come through God Himself speaking to an individual. The call can also be received through a vision or a dream. It can come through anointing by another prophet under the direction of the Holy Spirit. One does not take it upon himself to anoint and appoint a prophet of God. The commission comes from the Lord God Almighty.

When Moses was initially called to be a prophet of God, he asked the Lord for someone to speak for him. The Lord responded by appointing Aaron to speak for Moses. Somewhere along the line the Lord also anointed Miriam to speak as well. In the Book of Numbers scripture says, "Miriam and Aaron began to talk against Moses because of his Cushite wife." (Numbers 12:1) I believe, based on their boldness to criticize Moses, this scripture suggests Miriam and Aaron became proud of their roles as prophets.

It didn't appear the Lord had a problem with Moses's wife, but Miriam and Aaron did. God was still speaking to Moses and directing him. This indicates that the Lord was okay with the choices Moses had made. If there was a problem, God Himself would have spoken to Moses about it.

Consider the possibility that Miriam, Moses's older sister was the offender in this situation. Perhaps she was lecturing Aaron and pointing out the fact that Moses had married a Cushite. Maybe she was urging Aaron to confront Moses about this "violation." How do I know Miriam was the offender in this situation? I don't really, but if you read the scripture about this incident, the Lord only punished Miriam not Aaron. The Lord reprimanded both of them, but Miriam was the one punished.

The Lord uses flawed and imperfect people. I don't want to disillusion anyone, but there are no perfect people; God must use what He has-- the imperfect ones. He will decide what part of a person's life needs to be changed and when those changes should take place. That is not for the body of Christ to decide.

When someone comes to know Jesus as their Lord and Savior, people in the church almost always expect that person to change their life immediately. This newborn babe in Christ has much to learn and many worldly practices to address as he matures in his walk with the Lord. His language does not change overnight though there will be some in the body of Christ who will expect that. Perhaps this new babe in Christ is addicted to drugs, alcohol, pornography, sex, or gambling. You can't expect someone with these issues to become as pure as the driven snow overnight. Now God can and does transform people when they come to know Christ, but it usually takes a great deal of prayer and discipline for the Lord to complete the transformation. Correcting language or pulling people out of bondage can take years. I encourage you not to judge others, but look at your own life and be reminded of the things the Lord had to deal with in you. Love the new believer and encourage them. The Lord will direct this person in the things that must be changed and the order in which change will take place.

Aaron and Miriam began to say, "Has the Lord spoken only through Moses? Hasn't He also spoken through us?" (Numbers 12:2) Moses was a very humble man and this attack on Moses angered the Lord.

"At once the Lord said to Moses, Aaron and Miriam, 'Come out to the tent of meeting, all three of you.' So, the three of them went out. Then the Lord came down in a pillar of cloud; He stood at the entrance to the tent and summoned Aaron and Miriam." (Numbers 12:4)

I don't know about you, but if the Lord ever called me out like that my knees would be knocking; in fact, I would be shaking from head to toe! When one angers the Lord, and He decides that the offense warrants His direct intervention, one truly realizes what the term, "the wrath of the Lord" is all about.

"When the two stepped forward, He said, 'Listen to my words: When there is a prophet among you, I, the Lord, reveal myself to them in visions, I speak to them in dreams. But this is not true of my servant Moses; he is faithful in all my house.

With him I speak face to face, clearly and not in riddles; he sees the form of the Lord.'" (Numbers 12:6-8)

If you continue reading Numbers, Chapter 12, you will see that because the Lord was so angry, He afflicted Miriam with leprosy. He did not afflict Aaron; He only afflicted Miriam. Remember that Moses understood the power of God; he was humble before God. What did Moses do when Miriam became leprous? He was humble enough that Moses prayed to the Lord for mercy on behalf of Miriam, and the Lord healed her. God required her to remain in that condition for seven days, and she had to stay outside the camp until she had been cleansed. By requiring Miriam to stay leprous for seven days and to stay outside the camp, God was humbling Miriam. Moses could have been happy and gloated; he could have celebrated the fact the Lord stood with him against Aaron and Miriam. Instead, Moses prayed for

Miriam to be healed. We could all take a lesson from Moses's actions in this situation.

From this scripture we get a sense of how one knows he is a prophet of God and what defines him:

1. It is the Lord who appoints and anoints His prophets. No one can choose to be a messenger of God or be elected by others. God Himself will call you to be His voice to the body of Christ. You will know when you have been anointed and appointed to be a prophet because you will hear His call. Likewise, if you do not hear the Lord calling you to this office, you have not been called to be His prophet.

2. The Lord will reveal Himself in visions to the one He appoints to be His prophet.

    Let's look at Daniel, where he received revelation from the Lord in a vision. "At that time, I, Daniel, mourned for three weeks. I ate no choice food; no meat or wine touched my lips; and I used no lotions at all until the three weeks were over." (Daniel 10:2-3)

    Visions are powerful and as you read about the vision that Daniel had concerning the end times, you will see that it took all his strength away. The vision was very troubling to Daniel.

    When the meaning of his vision was given, the angel of the Lord had to strengthen Daniel before he could give the interpretation. Please note that Daniel fasted for three weeks while he sought the Lord for the meaning of this revelation. He did not withdraw from all food and drink, scripture says, "I ate no choice food; no meat or wine touched my lips." If I am interpreting this scripture correctly, he ate vegetables and drank water during this three-week period. There are many types of fasts, this is one. I caution you that unless God tells you specifically not to drink water during any fast that is longer than three days, you should be sure to drink plenty of water. The body can only go for three days without water before organs start to become affected. Of course, if God instructs you to withdraw from water, He will sustain you.

When a prophet receives a vision, he will often labor in prayer and fasting to receive the full meaning of what he has seen.

3. The Lord will speak to His prophet through dreams.

You should know that just having spiritual visions or dreams does not make someone a prophet. It is however, one indicator that a person is being called to be the voice of the Lord. You will recall when Pharaoh had a troubling dream, he called for the prophets to interpret his dream. The Pharaoh was not a prophet; instead, the prophets in this case were interpreters of the Pharaoh's dreams.

Not all visions and dreams come from the Holy Spirit. Some come from the enemy, and they are sent to cause great fear and to put people in bondage. I encourage you to seek the Lord for the meaning of any spiritual dream or vision you receive. Just as with Daniel, the Lord will send the meaning. You may need to do some fasting and praying to get the full meaning of what you have seen.

4. The Lord will speak face-to-face with His appointed prophet.

While the scripture says the Lord will speak face-to-face with His messenger, this might more clearly read mouth-to-mouth. The prophet hears the actual voice of the Lord. This is instead of an unconscious awareness of the Lord implanting words in his mind. The Word of God says that no man can see the face of God and live. In fact, He showed Moses His back when He passed by him in Exodus 33:19-20.

The Lord uses His prophets as His mouthpiece. In order to do this a prophet must be able to hear and recognize God's voice. He must also be able to have conversations with the Lord as Moses did. You will recall that Ezekiel (Ezekiel 4:14) and Peter (Acts 10:14) both objected when the Lord told them to defile themselves. God's anointed must be able to express their objections over the instruction they are hearing from the Lord. Prophets hear the voice of the Lord, but they also hear the voice of satan as well. In fact, all Christians hear satan at times. His voice brings temptation to which we can fall victim. Just as the Lord implants messages in our minds so can satan. Because of this, we must always verify what we are hearing is from God and not from the enemy. When a prophet hears something that seems to go against the Word of God, it is appropriate to go back to God and ask questions.

There are times when God's spokesmen do some very strange things at the Lord's direction. Isaiah walked around naked for three years at the Lord's direction (Isaiah 20:4). The Lord directed Hosea to marry a prostitute (Hosea 1:2). In both of these cases, you have to imagine that the people harassed and ridiculed them. Prophets must have thick skin and keep their eyes on the Lord who is directing them.

God requires obedience, but with His anointed ones, the Lord will allow them to argue their case before him. The Lord made an accommodation for Ezekiel when he objected to the Lord's instruction to cook his food over human excrement by allowing him instead to cook his food over animal dung (Ezekiel 4:14). It was a small accommodation, but an accommodation none the less.

5. The Lord visibly shows Himself to His appointed prophets. They see His form. This was a definitive confirmation that Moses was a prophet. Moses had this kind of a relationship because of the powerful way God used him.

6. The Lord will speak to His prophets clearly not in parables so they understand with nothing hidden.

Often God will explain to His anointed ones why things are happening or why things are going to happen. He does this so that the body of Christ can prepare for coming events. The prophet's role when revelation is given is to pray and intercede for the body of Christ and to understand how the Lord intends for a revelation to be used. There are times when a revelation is given only for the purpose of intercession. Other times revelation is to be spoken.

7.   Another vital function of the office of the prophet is obedience to the Holy Spirit when a message is given. One who stands in this office will speak the words the Lord gives him to speak. If God's messenger does not speak a word as directed by the Holy Spirit, the Lord will hold him accountable for not warning the people. Further, the prophet does not have a choice when it comes to confronting sin. When God's spokesman sees someone committing sin, it is his responsibility before God to address that sin. If God's anointed fails to address sin, he will be held accountable.

Ezekiel says, "Son of man, I have made you a watchman (another word for prophet) for the people of Israel; so, hear the word I speak and give them warning from Me. When I say to a wicked person, 'You will surely die,' and you do not warn them or speak out to dissuade them from their evil ways in order to save their life, that wicked person will die for their sin, and I will hold you (the prophet) accountable for their blood. But if you do warn the wicked person and they do not turn from their wickedness or from their evil ways, they will die for their sin; but you (the prophet) will have saved yourself." (Ezekiel 3:17-19)

The above scripture goes on to say, "When a righteous person turns from their righteousness and does evil, and I put a stumbling block before them, they will die. Since you (the prophet) did not warn them, they will die for their sin. The righteous things that person did will not be remembered, and I will hold you (the prophet) accountable for their blood. But if you do warn the righteous person not to sin and they do not sin, they will surely live because they took warning, and you will have saved yourself." (Ezekiel 3:20-21)

8.   The prophet's life is used by the Lord God Almighty as an example to His people. Another significant scripture when it

comes to defining a prophet is: "For I have made you a sign to the Israelites." (Ezekiel 12:6) In this scripture, the Lord had Ezekiel symbolically go into exile to demonstrate that the Lord was going to send the Israelites into exile for their sins. The Lord used the lives of His prophets many times as examples to the Lord's people. This is just one of those examples.

9.   A prophet is the messenger of the Lord. He speaks for God. The words spoken by the messenger of God are not from his own intellect or insights; rather, they are words spoken by God Himself through His spokesman. God's messenger is not significant in and of himself. The thing that makes God's messenger important is that he speaks the Lord's word to the people.

In scripture there are many words used to refer to a prophet of God. Prophets can be referred as a messenger, a spokesman, a seer, a mouthpiece, a watchman, God's anointed, God's chosen one, or God's servant.

I have listed all of these aspects of being a prophet to encourage those going through this study to look back over their lives. I have no doubt that there are people studying this subject who may have blocked the memory of the call the Lord placed upon their lives. There are many reasons this may have been done. Fear can cause people to ignore or block the Lord's call. Lack of faith can cause a person to ignore the Lord's call. There may be a feeling of unworthiness to serve in this office. This is the very type of person upon whom the Lord places His anointing and commission to serve in this office.

Those who intentionally refuse the anointing and commission will be dealt with by the Lord. Those who do not have the faith to believe that the Lord has called and anointed them are different from those who refuse the call and anointing. It is my hope and prayer that the Lord will refresh His call upon those who have lacked the faith to operate in this office in spite of the call and anointing to do so.

Questions for Study and Discussion

1. Who can operate through the manifestation gifts of the Holy Spirit?

2. Who was initially called to speak the Lord's word to the people of Israel?

3. Who said, "Hasn't the Lord also spoken through us?"

4. Who did God punish for speaking against Moses and how?

5. Who appoints and commissions prophets of God?

6. What methods does the Lord use when He communicates with a prophet?

7. What are the consequences when the prophet does not warn the people of their sin? Explain.

8. What is essential to know about the life of a prophet?

9. What makes the prophet important?

CHAPTER 3

THROUGH WHOM DOES THE LORD SPEAK?

Throughout the Old and New Testaments, you will find individuals who are known as prophets. There were male and female prophets. God does not look at gender when He appoints someone.

When someone is prophesying or operating through any of the manifestation gifts if you are looking at their gender, you personally have a problem. God spoke through a burning bush when He first spoke to Moses. (Exodus 3:2) He spoke through a donkey in Balaam's case. (Numbers 22:29) God will speak through whatever or whomever He chooses to speak. God does not look at the gender or the outward appearance of someone He appoints to be His messenger. He looks at their heart.

It is my opinion that husbands and wives who take their marriage vows before the Lord become one in the spirit as well as the flesh. God views the couple as one. Therefore, I believe an anointing upon one is an anointing upon both because they are one. In Mark the scripture says, "And the two will become one flesh. So, they are no longer two, but one flesh." (Mark 10:8) Now, there are some caveats to this. A prophet may come into the marriage having already been anointed and commissioned by the Holy Spirit. In this case, the spouse over time may receive the commission to operate in this office. Just as with Aaron and Moses, the call and commission remain strongest upon the individual who was initially commissioned by God. There are prophets whose spouses like Hosea's rejected the Lord altogether though married to a prophet. In situations such as this there would be no anointing upon the spouse. There will also be spouses who may not be willing to take up the call. In that case, the unwilling spouse will miss out on the blessing the Lord places upon His chosen ones.

The Lord called me to be a prophet in June of 1979 when He told me He was appointing me to be His mouthpiece to the body of Christ. He did not say the words, "I have chosen you to be a prophet." What He said described what a prophet does. He spoke to me directly after a very long period of repentance and rededication to Him. I did not see a vision at that time, and I did not have a dream. He spoke to me. It was Him! I had no doubt in my heart I had heard the voice of the Lord.

My response to Him was to say, "You want me to be your voice to the body of Christ? Lord why would You want to honor me in this way? Look at all I have done to violate Your holy Word, and Your will for my life. I have failed You in so many different ways. Yet, You are calling me to be Your voice to the body of Christ!" I humbly accepted His call but allowed Him the opportunity to withdraw His anointing from me when He recognized His mistake. Understand I was young and unfamiliar with how the Lord anoints His prophets. I know now that God does not make mistakes. He will speak through the humble one who is willing to be obedient to the Holy Spirit.

The confirmation of that call came the next Sunday when a message in tongues was given, and the Lord had me give the interpretation. That was the beginning of my ministry. It was on that day I understood by the power of the Holy Spirit, I would know when He wanted me to speak. I began to shake all over when the anointing of the Spirit came upon me. I experienced warmth flowing from the top of my head down over the rest of my body. I felt as if God Himself had placed His hands on my shoulders as evidenced by a very heavy pressure I experienced. There was no doubt I was to speak. As I opened my mouth in faith, the words began to flow. It was spontaneous, and it was the Holy Spirit giving me the words He wanted me to speak. Now, I had a lot to learn, but that was the start.

You might say this sounds like it was just a simple interpretation I spoke. Many people minister in that way. You would be correct; however, it was the power of the anointing I experienced that verified and confirmed the Lord's call upon me.

For many years after I was called by the Lord, I would not acknowledge He had actually called me to be a prophet. Remember Jesus is the true prophet. It is His words that are spoken when God's anointed one relays a message. Remember also, when the Lord initially called me, I gave Him permission to take His anointing back when He discovered His mistake. I am still confounded and amazed that He speaks through me the way He does, and He has never taken His anointing back.

When the Lord gives me a message for the body of Christ there isn't always a strong feeling. Often, I simply hear the word the Lord is speaking, and I repeat what I am hearing. Sometimes the feeling can be mild. Other times the feeling can be extremely strong.

No one should minister based upon a feeling. Some people who minister through the manifestation gifts never feel anything. We minister by faith out of obedience. However, when a believer is just starting to operate through the gifts of the Holy Spirit, there can be a very intense feeling simply to verify and confirm it is the Holy Spirit.

If someone comes to you and says the Lord has directed that they anoint you to be a prophet of God, be skeptical. Don't simply accept what has been spoken to you. While the Lord may send another prophet to anoint and appoint you to serve in this office, once that anointing and appointment has occurred, the Holy Spirit will send confirmation after confirmation for that anointing. Unless you receive confirmation from the Lord proceed with caution. I have seen people in the body of Christ who are not themselves prophets, going around placing an anointing upon others to serve effectively in the office of the prophet,. This can cause confusion both in the individual who has been anointed, and in the body of Christ when this person attempts to minister in this office without a true anointing from the Holy Spirit.

God spoke directly to Moses, Samuel, and many other prophets when they were called. Samuel was directed by God to anoint Saul and then David. Neither of these men knew they were chosen by God until Samuel anointed and commissioned them in the name of the Lord. Joseph's commission came through a spiritual dream.

It is the prophet's obligation to speak what the Lord has spoken exactly as the word was given without adding any of his own opinions or agendas; but his obligation does not end there. It is the obligation of God's anointed one to pray and intercede on behalf of an individual, a body of believers, or even a nation to act upon the word the Lord has spoken through him. However, the prophet cannot make an individual believer or a body of believers act on the word the Lord has spoken. The Lord uses His prophet to give wise counsel, but again the Lord's messenger cannot make those believers receive that counsel and act upon it.

God spoke to Moses when He commissioned him saying, "I am sending you to Pharaoh to bring My people the Israelites out of Egypt." (Exodus 3:10) How many times did Moses have to go to Pharaoh before he actually let the people go? Much tragedy could have been avoided if Pharaoh would have just obeyed the first time Moses appeared before him.

Jeremiah was told by God, "Do not say to me, 'I am too young.' You must go to everyone I send you to and say whatever I command you. Do not be afraid of them, for I am with you and will rescue you, declares the Lord." (Jeremiah 1:7-8) God appointed Ezekiel to be His prophet by saying, "Son of man, stand up on your feet and I will speak to you. As He spoke, the Spirit came into me and raised me to my feet, and I heard Him speaking to me. He said: 'Son of man, I am sending you to the Israelites.'" (Ezekiel 2:1-3)

God called the apostle Paul (whose name was Saul at the time he was called) and commissioned him as an apostle and prophet in Acts. God actually told Ananias not Paul that He had called Paul. Read it yourself, God told Ananias, "Go! This man is My chosen instrument to proclaim My name to the Gentiles and their kings and to the people of Israel. I will show him how much he must suffer for My name.

Then Ananias went to the house and entered it. Placing his hands on Saul, he said, 'Brother Saul, the Lord Jesus, who appeared to you on the road while you were coming here, has sent me so that you may see again and be filled with the Holy Spirit.'" (Acts 9:15-17)

The ministry of God's anointed is more than simply communicating a message. Examining the lives of prophets like Moses, Ezekiel, Elijah, Elisha and Hosea will teach you that being a prophet is not a popular way of life. If you are seeking to win friends and influence people, being a messenger of God is not the way to go. Then again, one cannot decide to be a prophet or be elected to serve as one. Prophets are chosen and anointed by God.

God's anointed ones throughout the Bible have been required by God to pray for and address the wrongs of a nation, warn the nation of the coming wrath of the Lord, confront kings who had sinned and disobeyed God, live in hiding because people wanted to hunt them down to kill them, marry a prostitute, lay on one side for many days while eating food that was cooked over animal dung Ezekiel 4:14.

Questions for Study and Discussion

1. Discuss through whom the Lord speaks.

2. Discuss the special bond between the prophet and their spouse.

3. Discuss the various methods used by the Lord to anoint and commission His prophets.

4. When the Lord directs a prophet to place the commission and anointing upon someone to minister in the office of the prophet, how does that prophet know it is from the Lord?

5. It is the obligation of the prophet to speak what the Lord has spoken to him. Does his obligation end there? Explain.

CHAPTER 4

THE BAPTISM OF THE HOLY SPIRIT

Before we can actually study about the office of the prophet, we need to discuss one of the main tools necessary a believer must have to be able to function in the office of the prophet. That is the infilling or baptism of the Holy Spirit.

Acts 2:1-4 says, "When the day of Pentecost came, they were all together in one place. Suddenly a sound like the blowing of a violent wind came from heaven and filled the whole house where they were sitting. They saw what seemed to be tongues of fire that separated and came to rest on each of them. All of them were filled with the Holy Spirit and began to speak in other tongues as the Spirit enabled them."

I have never heard anyone teach this before, but here goes. As I have meditated on these verses of scriptures, I believe the Lord showed me through the Spirit what happened in that upper room. The scripture above mentions that it looked like tongues of fire were resting upon each one in the upper room. I believe what they were seeing was what goes on in the spiritual realm when someone receives the Holy Spirit into their lives.

Any time God opens the spirit realm through visions or dreams, it is the gift of discerning of spirits in operation. This is one of the manifestation gifts of the Holy Spirit. There is much more to this gift than just giving the believer a glimpse into the spirit realm, but I believe that is why those in the upper room were seeing what looked like tongues of fire. Tongues of fire do not usually appear over a person who is receiving the baptism of the Holy Spirit, at least not in the physical realm. Something like that only happens when the curtain separating this world from the realm of the Spirit is rolled back. Understand, this is the record of when the Holy Spirit was initially given, and it made an impression on those who were waiting on the Lord. Many of the manifestation gifts of the Holy Spirit were present and operating when this baptism occurred. If you read Acts, Chapter 2, you will be able to identify many of the manifestation gifts operating in that chapter.

When the Spirit was given on that day, there was a sound like a mighty rushing wind. Imagine a powerful tornado blowing through and the noise that would make. The wind of the Spirit can be much louder than the noise created by nature! All the people were speaking in many languages at the top of their voices, at the same time. These were languages they had never learned. I would venture to say that when they were infused with the Holy Spirit, there was extreme supernatural power flowing, and very strong feelings that went along with that power as the Holy Spirit entered into each of those people.

Peter (the one who had denied Jesus three times) got up and began to speak. I believe he was speaking under the power of the Holy Spirit, through the manifestation of the gift of a word of knowledge as he declared this was what Jesus had promised them. The Comforter, the Holy Spirit, would have eased the pain of the loss we all feel when someone dies. Yes, Jesus was raised to life again, but He was also taken from them.

Scripture says there were around 120 people in the upper room when the Holy Spirit was given, and all of them began to speak in other tongues as the Spirit gave them the ability to do so. He did not fill just some of those people; no one was left out. All the people who had been waiting in that upper room were baptized in the Holy Spirit and they all spoke in other tongues. That is one of the reasons the gift of speaking in tongues is sometimes referred to as the evidence of having received the baptism in the Holy Spirit. When this scripture says, "They began to speak in other tongues as the Spirit enabled them," I imagine when those tongues rested upon each believer, that is when they were infused with power, and the gift of tongues began to operate. This is what the Lord impressed upon me as I meditated on these scriptures.

I was raised in the in Church of God. Not the Pentecostal Church of God; it was the Evangelical church. The church my family belonged to was headquartered in Anderson, Indiana. Many great gospel singers, writers, and even Christian politicians came out of that church.

The Church of God believed and taught that all people are born in sin; and therefore, all needed to be saved when they reached an age of accountability. They believed in water baptism; they believed in the sacrament of communion, and they believed in the literal practice of foot washing, which was practiced at a service held each year on the Thursday before Good Friday. Over the years, this practice has all but disappeared due to the potential for passing diseases. At the last foot washing service I attended, instead of a basin of water and a long towel wrapped around someone's waist, they used disposable and sanitized wet towels purchased from a medical supply store. It just felt like something was missing from that service. However, the point behind foot washing is not really to clean someone's feet. This practice is observed as a sign that we identify with Jesus and His suffering. It is also a practice of deep humility. The Church of God taught many good things, but they did not teach about the baptism of the Holy Spirit, nor did they teach about the manifestation gifts. They did, teach the humility that must be present to minister for the Lord in any way, including ministering through any of manifestation gifts.

My father thought that the Pentecostal church was radical and misguided. I will admit that because of the way many of these churches have allowed the Spirit to move so freely in their services over past years, people outside of the Pentecostal Church were afraid to even visit one of them. Outsiders did not understand the freedom of the Holy Spirit they practiced. People became fearful and even alarmed when the dancing started, and people started falling under the power of God. I don't know why people have such a fear of the Holy Spirit. It's not like we practice handling poisonous snakes as is practiced in some churches! Anyway, my father was sure speaking in tongues was from satan, and he called those who attended the Pentecostal churches "Holy Rollers."

When my twin sister Judy and I were about 15 years old, we became disheartened with the specific Church of God we were attending, and we started looking for another church. We had a friend who was a member of the Assembly of God Church and she invited us to visit her church. When my father found out that we were attending a Pentecostal church, he told us that if we ever came home speaking in tongues, we could find another place to live. He felt like this in spite of the scriptures that taught about how the Holy Spirit was given after Jesus was taken up into heaven.

Most churches do not teach about the baptism of the Holy Spirit and they do not teach or recognize the ministry of the manifestation gifts in their services. That is probably because they do not understand these gifts or how they operate. That doesn't mean these people are not Christians, it just means they lack the knowledge of these gifts and the open-mindedness to learn about them.

Once an individual accepts Christ as their Savior, and they begin to read the Bible and learn about the things of God, they become aware of the requirement to be baptized in water. For some believers, that will be as far as they go.

Some churches teach that water baptism is required for a person to go to heaven when they die. However, the thief on the cross was never baptized in water. As he was dying on the cross, he reached out to Jesus. Let's think about the thief on the cross, he didn't actually pray the "sinner's prayer." He asked that Jesus remember him when He came into His kingdom. Jesus said that day he would be with Him in Paradise. The closest thing I find to a sinner's prayer in the Bible is Romans 10:9-10 that says, "If you declare with your mouth, 'Jesus is Lord,' and believe in your heart that God raised Him from the dead, you will be saved." That is not actually a prayer in my opinion; it is a declaration.

Many churches today do not even teach about being baptized with water, let alone being baptized in the Holy Spirit. Let's be very clear, neither of these baptisms are required for a person to be saved and go to heaven, and there is no set order for these baptisms to happen in a believer's life.

When someone prays to receive the baptism of the Holy Spirit, the Spirit comes to reside within them, and when He does, He brings all His manifestation gifts with Him to be used as needed. I know that this is not how many people interpret the scriptures, but think of it like this: When you go to buy a car, you don't buy the steering wheel separately, and you expect that the tires will be included in the purchase as well. When a person opens themselves to receive the Holy Spirit, they get all of Him; the manifestation gifts are part of the package that comes with the Holy Spirit.

The Holy Spirit is a gentleman; He does not force Himself upon anyone. The gifts are activated by faith out of obedience and, "The Spirit distributes as He wills." (I Corinthians 12:11) While it is not a requirement for someone to be baptized in the Holy Spirit, I feel that each believer should study and seek to receive everything that is available from God. Including all nine of the fruits that enter us as a seed when we are saved. The fruit of the Spirit can be found in Galatians 5:22-23.

Once someone receives Jesus, they are saved and the baptism of the Holy Spirit, is available to them. I have seen people while at the altar to receive Jesus, then pray to receive the Holy Spirit, and they walk away from the altar having received salvation and the Holy Spirit, with the evidence of speaking in tongues. Yes, it is possible to receive both experiences at the same time. People can make a big thing about receiving the Holy Spirit, but it is just not that complicated.

The believer must yield to the Spirit and open their mouth in faith and begin to speak. I have seen and heard of people being baptized in water, and they open themselves at the same time to the Holy Spirit. When they do that, they often come up out of the water speaking in tongues. In essence, they received both baptisms at the same time. Water baptism can be a very powerful experience, especially when the baptism of the Holy Spirit is received at the same time. What an experience to remember! This can happen; one only needs to yield to the Spirit.

When receiving the baptism of the Holy Spirit, the mouth does not take off speaking uncontrollably on its own. We must give voice to the gift of tongues. Tongues is also known as a "heavenly language" or a "prayer language." Please understand, one must yield to the Holy Spirit to speak in tongues. When we speak English or any other learned language, our mouths do not just talk mindlessly on their own do they? No, we must will our mouth to speak as we give voice to what we want to say. Speaking in tongues is like speaking a new language we have never before learned, but we are always in control of our mouth. Tongues doesn't just come blasting out of our mouths uncontrollably.

After someone asks the Lord to baptize them in the Holy Spirit, they should then start lifting their voice to the Lord in praise and worship. The heavenly language will begin to flow as this is done. We must yield to the Spirit and speak in faith.

There came a time when my sister and I were attending a youth rally for the Assembly of God Church. Thousands of young people were in attendance. These rallies usually included an entire church service aimed at the youth. When the altar call was given, I responded. As I was standing at the altar, I began to pray. I said something like this: "God you know how my father feels about this, but if this Holy Spirit experience is real, and it is not from the devil, but from you; I want to receive it."

I stood there in the midst of what seemed to be a sea of young people. I put my arms around myself and just began to praise God. As I did that, I opened myself to the Holy Spirit and before I knew it, I was praying in tongues. It was such a pleasant and comforting experience that I just continued to pray in my new "prayer language." To be honest, I was actually afraid to stop because I didn't want this wonderful gift to go away.

Understand, I didn't know much about the baptism of the Holy Spirit when I prayed to receive Him. I continued to pray in the Spirit, but not out loud; rather, it was my spirit reaching out to God in tongues. For the entire ride home, I was praying in tongues. When we arrived home, I went straight to my room, but I didn't go to sleep, I just wanted to pray in tongues. I finally fell asleep and when I awakened in the morning, I was pleasantly surprised to realize that this wonderful gift was still with me. This was an experience I could not share with my parents until many years later. I did not even tell my twin sister; I was pretty sure she would go and blab to my parents, and I would be out in the cold.

I was married and out of the house before I got up the courage to open up about receiving the Holy Spirit. My mother many years later as she was praying for her dying mother, found herself praying in tongues. I was the first person she called!

She told my dad at some point, he was not happy, but he couldn't kick her out. He was a godly man, and speaking in tongues was not a scriptural reason for divorce! He mellowed over the years as he realized that my mom was still the same person she was before she started praying in tongues.

I am sharing this because I want you to know, my dad knew the Lord. He testified to others when given the opportunity. He prayed with people to receive the Lord as their Savior, but speaking in tongues was a step too far for him. Another reason I have related this experience from my life is to make this point: It is okay if the thought of receiving the Holy Spirit and speaking in tongues makes you uncomfortable, but He is available to all who will receive Him. I do think it is important to know about the Holy Spirit and all of His workings, even if you are not open to receiving the Holy Spirit for yourself.

When ministering through any of the manifestation gifts it is important to realize we are not ministering on our own, it is an operation of the Holy Spirit and He gets the credit and glory for what He has said or done through us. Our God will not allow His people to steal His glory. Remember that pride goes before a fall.

If a believer begins to feel like they are better than their brothers and sisters in the Lord because they have received the Holy Spirit and have the manifestation gifts operating in them, just keep in mind God can humble people in very unimaginable but effective ways.

Questions for Study and Discussion

1. Can a person be saved and go to heaven without being baptized in water?

2. Is the baptism in the Holy Spirit required for a person to be saved and go to heaven?

3. Is there a specific order for water baptism and the baptism of the Holy Spirit to occur in a believer's life?

4. When a believer is filled with the Holy Spirit, is the gift of tongues uncontrollable?

5. What are the two ways the manifestation gifts of the Holy Spirit operate within the believer?

CHAPTER 5

RESPONDING TO THE HOLY SPIRIT

I encourage everyone when they sense the Holy Spirit speaking to write down what the Spirit says. Keep a notebook of messages you have received. When the Spirit speaks, He often speaks the same word to others in the congregation. This serves to confirm that what the believer has heard is coming directly from the Lord. It may be that a word given in a service is the same message the Lord spoke to another believer who wrote it down outside of a service. If this happens to you, consider this a confirmation from the Holy Spirit that you are hearing from the Lord. When I say the same word, I mean the same subject. The exact words used will usually differ but the theme of the message will be the same.

From time to time, review the words you have received and written. If what the Lord has spoken, is being repeated over and over again to you, as can happen when you first start hearing from the Holy Spirit, ask Him why that message keeps coming. It may be the Lord speaking directly to you about something He wants you to change in your own life.

The Lord used many different methods to give messages to His people throughout scripture. Words we receive from the Lord must be received through one of those methods documented in scripture. Sometimes He just dropped a word into a believer's mind. He spoke through dreams or visions in the scriptures. On one occasion, the Spirit Himself wrote a message on a wall using what appeared to be a human hand, there was no body attached to the hand. He spoke directly to some of His prophets. Moses heard the voice of the Lord as did Noah, Jonah, and Abraham, just to name a few. He sent angels to speak the word of the Lord to others. Since any message we receive must comply with the Bible, be sure the method by which you receive a word agrees with scripture. If the method used to deliver a message is not found in scripture, question if it is a message from the Lord. Remember that satan has counterfeits. It is important that what we are hearing is from the Holy Spirit.

The Lord always gives confirmation for what we are hearing. The first confirmation should be the Bible. If it agrees with the Bible, ask the Lord how He wants the word to be handled. If what you are hearing is not scriptural, reject it and let it go. Other confirmations include hearing the same word from other people. You may hear the same message through a sermon. When that happens, you know you are hearing from the Holy Spirit.

A word might be a specific and personal message for the one who received it. Other times it might not be a word from the Lord at all. In I John 4:1-3 it says, "Beloved, do not believe every spirit, but test the spirits to see whether they are from God. For many false prophets have gone out into the world. This is how you can recognize the Spirit of God: Every spirit that acknowledges Jesus Christ has come in the flesh is from God, but every spirit that does not acknowledge Jesus, is not from God."

Be aware, satan has a counterfeit for all of the manifestations of the Holy Spirit. That is why it is important to validate and confirm what you have received.

When Moses went to the Pharoah with the miraculous powers God had given him, the magicians were able to duplicate many of those wonders. Believers, especially those new to the things of the Spirit, must be careful. Don't be deceived by responding to voices that do not come from the Holy Spirit. Everything that comes from the Holy Spirit must agree with the Word of God. If your message points to another god, or says something that does not agree with scripture, it is false prophecy.

The mere occurrence of speaking in "other tongues," or any other supernatural manifestation, is not uncontestable evidence of the work and presence of the Spirit. Speaking in tongues can be counterfeited by human initiative or demonic activity as in other religions. The Bible cautions us not to believe every spirit, but to examine whether our spiritual experiences really do come from God.

In order to be valid, speaking in tongues must be enabled by the Holy Spirit. To follow the norm in the Book of Acts, speaking a message in tongues will be the spontaneous prompting of the Holy Spirit. It is not a learned wonder, nor can it be taught by instructing believers to speak in incoherent syllables.

In II Thessalonians 2:9, the Holy Spirit explicitly warns that in the last days there will be within the church hypocrisy, signs and wonders from satanic powers, and deceitful workers disguising themselves as God's servants. We must heed these warnings about counterfeit spiritual manifestations and signs. If someone claiming to speak in tongues is not committed to the Lord Jesus Christ and the authority of scripture, and is not attempting to obey God's Word, whatever manifestations he or she may have, are not from the Spirit of the Living God.

Anyone ministering in the Spirit must operate in faith and love. When I get a word from the Lord, I will include the scriptures in my copy of what I give from the pulpit, for lack of time I don't usually give the scriptures when I speak the word. If anyone questions what I have spoken, I have the proof texts that I can give them. Even spontaneous words must be quickly checked before giving them.

The things taking place in the service can confirm the word the Lord has given. Often times the pastor's message, will be on the same subject of the word the Lord has given through me. The pastor may use some of the same scriptures that are in what the Spirit has given through me. There was a time when, I was given a flyer as I came into church. The flyer contained some of the exact words the Lord had given me before I got to service. That was a confirmation I was hearing from the Lord, and that the word I had received was for that service.

Because I speak so frequently, I usually notify the one in charge of the service that I have a word before the service so that he can give me the opportunity to minister. We do not collaborate with each other before the service. What I mean by that is the pastors do not ask me what I have to say and I don't usually tell them. We have all ministered together long enough that we know the Spirit is in control.

For those just beginning to operate in these gifts, the pastor may ask to hear the message before it is given in the service. Be prepared to tell him the topic or give a snapshot of what you have received.

There are times I don't receive a word even after seeking the Lord all week, and that is okay. II Peter 1:21-22 says, "Above all, we must understand that no prophecy of scripture comes from one's own interpretation. For no such prophecy was ever brought forth by the will of man, but men spoke from God as they were carried along by the Holy Spirit." I will never speak a word from my own spirit and place the Lord's name to it. His anointing is too important to me. His anointing would be lifted very quickly if I even considered doing that.

It is my obligation as a prophet to seek the Lord. Anyone who has been filled with the Spirit can seek Him for a word. He doesn't have to give me or anyone else a word; He is God after all. I love it when the Lord gives a word through someone else in the congregation. It does my heart good when someone steps out in obedience to the Holy Spirit to give a word they have received.

As a person yields to the Spirit, they will develop a presentation style. No one should copy the presentation method someone else uses. As each individual allows the Spirit to minister through them, a presentation style will emerge. An important suggestion I would offer is that when speaking for the Lord, it is good to state that it is the Lord speaking.

The method I use when presenting a word from the Lord is to say something like, "The Lord would say." I always try to end a word by saying, "Says the Lord."

Questions for Study and Discussion

1. When anyone senses the Holy Spirit speaking, what should they do?

2. Discuss some of the methods the Holy Spirit will use to impart a word to a believer.

3. If you believe you are hearing a word from the Lord, but it is not through a method that the Holy Spirit used in scripture, what should you do?

4. Should you believe every voice that you hear speaking a word into your spirit? Why or why not?

5. If someone speaking in tongues is not committed to the Lord Jesus Christ, and the authority of scriptures, and is not attempting to obey God's Word, should you believe them when they speak a message? Please explain.

6. Can a man speak a word of prophecy out of his own will? Please explain.

CHAPTER 6

PREREQUISITES TO SERVING AS A PROPHET OF GOD

There are a few prerequisites for operating in the office of the prophet of God.

1. The most significant prerequisite to operating in the office of the prophet is that God Himself must place an anointing upon an individual. That anointing will be accompanied by a commission or appointment from God to serve in this office. No one can operate as a prophet without this anointing and appointment.

2. You must be born again. Most people interested in this topic have already asked Jesus into their hearts. Otherwise, you would not be studying the office of the prophet. Scripture says, "If you declare with your mouth, 'Jesus is Lord,' and believe in your heart that God raised him from the dead, you will be saved." (Romans 10:9) There are two parts to becoming a Christian. You must profess with your mouth, and believe in your heart that He is alive.

    There are some religions that recognize Jesus as a prophet, but they do not recognize Him as the Son of God. Many people think that simply stating Jesus is Lord seals the deal. It does not! One must also believe in his heart that Jesus is the Son of God and that God raised Him from the dead. Without that belief in your heart, you cannot be saved. In case there is someone who has not received Jesus as their Lord and Savior, I want to give you that opportunity right now. I invite you to pray this simple prayer in faith believing in your heart.

Dear Heavenly Father, I believe that Jesus Christ is the Son God, your only Son, and I believe that God raised Jesus from the dead. I accept Jesus as my Lord and Savior. I invite Jesus to come into my heart right now. Forgive all my sins, and cleanse me from all unrighteousness. Help me to live for you and demonstrate to others the love and mercy of God. Thank you for the change that your presence will make in me. In Jesus name I pray. Amen.

3. To effectively operate in the office of the prophet, one must be filled with the Holy Spirit of God. Acts tells about the baptism of the Holy Spirit. If you read this scripture it says, "And they were all filled with the Holy Spirit, and began to speak with other tongues as the Spirit enabled them." (Acts 2:4)

There may be people going through this teaching who do not feel it is necessary to speak in tongues. That's okay. Prophets in the Old Testament did not have this gift. It is a free gift of God, but He does not force anyone to receive any of His gifts. Often those who do not believe in speaking in tongues do not understand this gift or how it operates. There are some individuals who are afraid of this gift, and have closed their minds to its operation in their own lives. Also, I have to say that I have seen this gift operating incorrectly from time to time in the church. If the gift of tongues is operating incorrectly in a body, believers and unbelievers can become confused and afraid.

The baptism of the Holy Spirit is much more than speaking in tongues. The baptism of the Holy Spirit infuses the believer with the power of God. It also opens the believer's heart and spiritual ears to the voice of the Lord.

One of the greatest benefits of the gift of speaking in tongues is the way the Holy Spirit uses this gift in intercessory prayer. The Lord calls His people to pray for situations and circumstances they don't know about. The Spirit that is within the believer can pray the perfect prayer to the Father bypassing their human intellect through the gift of tongues. These are not prayers that require interpretation.

These prayers of intercession could be offered to prevent wars, save someone's life, or to move God's hand on behalf of a nation. There are many other reasons why the Holy Spirit inspires believers to intercede.

We will discuss in this study that there are nine manifestation gifts of the Holy Spirit some are necessary to minister as a prophet, but the gift of speaking in tongues and the gift of interpretation of tongues are not required to operate in the life of a prophet of God.

If speaking in tongues were a prerequisite to operating in this office, many churches across the world would be without prophets. This is because many churches do not recognize or allow the gift of tongues to operate in the church today.

4. To operate effectively in the office of the prophet one must be able to recognize the voice of the Lord. Having the infilling of the Holy Spirit makes it easier to hear the voice of God, but there is no hard fast rule that one must have the infilling of the Holy Spirit to hear the voice of the Lord. It is the Lord who draws the unbeliever to come to him. Sometimes it is through the Holy Spirit speaking directly to the unbeliever that gets his attention, and he responds to the Lord. The more time one spends in the Lord's presence the easier it will be to distinguish the Lord's voice. Since the voice of the Lord is evidenced in many different ways, the prophet will be taught through the Holy Spirit when the Lord is speaking and what to do with what he has heard.

Questions for Study and Discussion

1. There are four prerequisites to operating in the office of the prophet, what are they?

2. What two manifestation gifts of the Holy Spirit were not in operation in the Old Testament?

3. Are the manifestation gifts of speaking in tongues and the gift of interpretation of tongues required to be operating in someone who is a prophet?

4. What is one of the greatest benefits of the gift of speaking in tongues?

CHAPTER 7

THE MANIFESTATION GIFTS
TOOLS FOR THE PROPHET

While one does not need to be a prophet to operate through the manifestation gifts, prophets use these gifts of the Holy Spirit as tools allowing them to effectively operate in the office of the prophet.

All prophets operate through the gift of prophecy, but they also operate through the revelation gifts. The operation of these particular manifestation gifts of the Holy Spirit is essential for a prophet of God. Some very powerful prophets also operate through the power gifts as well. For God's anointed, these gifts are used to accomplish the Lord's purposes, and prophets are very receptive to these gifts. I should add that not everyone who operates through these manifestation gifts is a prophet. Remember that only those who have been anointed and appointed by God are true prophets.

There is much mystery surrounding the manifestation gifts of the Holy Spirit. Many believers have preconceived ideas of what the manifestation gifts are and how they operate. There is a mistaken idea that the manifestation gifts are only for public ministry, and for this reason the operation of these gifts is many times ignorcd. The manifestation gifts have a private operation, and it is often a more significant side.

One of the greatest benefits to the private operation of the manifestation gifts is the strength that is built, and the closeness that develops between the Holy Spirit and the believer as these gifts operate time after time.

"When the day of Pentecost came, they were all together in one place. Suddenly a sound like the blowing of a violent wind came from heaven and filled the whole house where they were sitting. They saw what seemed to be tongues of fire that separated and came to rest on each of them. All of them were filled with the Holy Spirit and began to speak in other tongues as the Spirit enabled them." (Acts 2:1-4)

Once an individual accepts Christ as his Savior and receives the infilling of the Holy Spirit, the manifestation gifts are resident within the believer. The gifts are activated by faith out of obedience and, "He distributes to each one, just as He determines." (I Corinthians 12:11) Any Spirit-filled believer may find themselves called upon to minister through one or more of the manifestation gifts in a public service. We are merely vessels through which the Holy Spirit chooses to operate. It is a matter of yielding and obeying when His anointing is on us to minister.

I have to say that for me, it is always emotional when the Lord places His hand upon me to minister through these gifts. I personally feel very inadequate to have the Lord of all creation speak through me.

I have been asked how I know when the anointing is present. That anointing comes with unmistakable feelings. There are some people who simply have a strong assurance that what they are hearing is from the Spirit of God. The anointing can be enhanced and it can actually be activated through praise and worship. We never worship the gifts; we always worship the giver of the gifts.

The manifestation gifts of the Holy Spirit are supernatural and come from God's throne. These gifts have nothing to do with evil practices such as satanism, witchcraft, divination, fortune telling or any other evil practice. Neither is magic, or illusion involved in the operation of these gifts. The Holy Spirit does not use deception or tricks when He operates.

If you are ever in a church service or even alone praying, and your heart begins to pound like it might come out of your chest, and you begin to feel shaking that seems to be coming from inside of you, I would encourage you to pay attention. I have experienced a comforting warmth flowing over me. I have felt pressure on my shoulders. These are just some of the ways the Holy Spirit gets our attention and confirms that what we are hearing is from Him. While no specific feeling is necessary to have one of the manifestation gifts operate in your life, many times a very strong feeling will precede the operation; this is especially true when ministering in a public meeting. Listen to what the Spirit is speaking to you. Then evaluate what you are hearing. Is it scriptural? If you are in a service determine if it is in line with what is going on in the service. These are confirmations that the Holy Spirit is speaking to you.

When I first started ministering for the Lord, I had never heard about the anointing I have described to you. People never talked about the power of the anointing nor what that feels like; it was quite overwhelming for me. I hesitated to even talk about this because the anointing is so very personal, and it must be treated with reverence. These feelings were so strong I felt I needed to hold on to something. At the very beginning of my ministry, those feelings could last for hours after I ministered. Now days, there is often just a strong assurance of the Lord's presence when the anointing comes upon me to minister. I have also experienced pain as I have received a word of knowledge for someone the Spirit wanted to touch for healing.

These feelings can serve to simply validate that the Lord is present in a service. We should never minister just because we are feeling something. However, these feelings can be one of the ways the Holy Spirit gets our attention and confirms that we are hearing from Him.

Listen for the Lord. If you are hearing a voice, ask yourself if what you are hearing is scriptural? Is it in line with what is going on in the service? The answer to these questions can confirm that the Holy Spirit wants to speak through you.

These feelings lessen over time. After ministering for more than 40 years, I know when the Holy Spirit is prompting me to speak, but the feelings are not nearly as strong as when I first began operating through these gifts. It may be that initially, these feelings bolster a person's faith to minister when they are first starting out.

The anointing is powerful, but we can control what we do and say when that anointing is upon us. These feelings are a physical response to what is happening in the spiritual realm. I repeat, it is not necessary to feel anything when the Holy Spirit speaks through someone.

It is important that a believer who ministers through the manifestation gifts pay attention to how they are living their life. This is something that I have had to be very careful about in my own life. People are watching how we live even if we don't know it. If the words of the Lord are going to come out of your mouth, scripture says that, we must keep our lips from speaking any kind of evil. We must not gossip, use profane language, or take the Lord's name in vain. (I Peter 3:10) Now, we are all human and we make mistakes. So, before going into a service where the Holy Spirit may want to minister through us, it is important that we confess any sin, repent and turn away from any wrong, so we are in a position for the Holy Spirit to minister in and through us.

If you are holding an offense against someone, repent and release forgiveness or the Holy Spirit cannot effectively minister through you. God says of those who speak under the anointing of His Holy Spirit: "If you repent, I will restore you that you may serve Me; if you utter worthy, not worthless words, you will be My spokesman." (Jeremiah 15:19)

Romans 11:29 says, "For the gifts and the calling of God are irrevocable." It is a single verse of scripture but it is very important. This verse is saying that when God calls and commissions someone, the gifts that come along with that call and commission are never taken away, nor will the calling be taken away. Even if that person walks away from God, He has still given His gifts through His Holy Spirit, and His call is still upon that person. It is His desire that we confess our sins and repent so that we can be restored.

This is exactly what happened with King David when he sinned with Bathsheba. Peter was also called and anointed; he had worked miracles, but he denied Christ three times the night Jesus was betrayed. Both of these men were called by God; and they operated under the anointing of the Holy Spirit. They turned from God's path, and when they repented, they were restored. After God humbled them, He used them again in mighty and powerful ways. Knowing this should give everyone hope.

I want to caution if you are in a service where the Holy Spirit gifts are not welcome to operate, you should not speak in the service. What you are hearing may simply be confirming what is taking place in the service is from the Lord. It also may be a call for you to intercede concerning what is taking place in the service. Do not operate through any of the manifestation gifts in a service unless those gifts are accepted by the leadership.

When operating through the manifestation gifts it is crucial to operate in love. We must recognize we do not operate the gifts on our own, it is an operation of the Holy Spirit, and He gets the credit and glory for what has been done. Our God will not allow a believer to accept glory that belongs to the Lord. Remember pride goes before a fall.

When the Holy Spirit moves upon a person to operate through the manifestation gifts, it is because He has recognized a willing vessel. He will use those who are willing, humble in heart, and obedient to do what the Holy Spirit is telling them to do.

The Holy Spirit is very sensitive, and the anointing can be lifted quickly based on what is going on in a service. It is imperative that leadership cultivate a welcoming atmosphere so the Holy Spirit is motivated to operate in a service. The move of the Holy Spirit can be enhanced, and the anointing of the Holy Spirit can actually be activated through praise and worship. Likewise, if people are talking loudly in the sanctuary while worship is taking place, it can prevent the anointing from being manifested. Any large disruption during the time the Holy Spirit might make Himself known in the service can prevent Him from ministering. Turn your cell phone off!

A believer who ministers through the manifestation gifts must pay attention to how he is living his life and the words he allows to come from his mouth. If you desire to minister, you must keep your lips from speaking any kind of evil. You must not gossip, use profane language or take the Lord's name in vain. Now, we are all human, and we all make mistakes. So, before going into a service where the Holy Spirit may want to use you, be sure you are right with the Lord. Repent for any sins and ask the Lord to purify you. Then make yourself available to Him.

There is one last point that needs to be made about the operation of any of the manifestation gifts in a service; this applies to those operating in the office of the prophet as well. There is an order in the body of Christ that must be respected. Anyone operating through the manifestation gifts is under the authority of the person in charge of the meeting. Do not interrupt something that is already going on in a service to minister through these gifts. Wait for a break in the service and then speak.

If the person in charge of the service tells you to be quiet, you should stop speaking. If you have questions, go to that leader after the service to discuss the situation. If the one in charge of the meeting is out of touch with the Holy Spirit, the Lord will deal with him. God is not the author of confusion, and when no one takes charge of a service, things can quickly get out of hand. The Lord will honor your obedience in being willing to speak, even if you are not given the opportunity.

When you are just starting to minister, you may get so excited about receiving a word that your timing could be wrong. The message may not be for the service you are in but for a future service. If that is the case, the Lord will give you direction.

While preparing this study it became obvious that there is a great deal of confusion in the body of Christ concerning the gifts the Holy Spirit bestows upon His people. In an attempt to clear some of the confusion let's talk about the various types of gifts and their purposes. There are three categories of gifts that the Holy Spirit places within His people: ministry gifts, motivational gifts, and manifestation gifts. Since the manifestation gifts are tools used by prophets, each one of them will be discussed and defined in this study. Any believer who has been filled with the Holy Spirit has the manifestation gifts resident within him. These gifts become operational when a believer steps out in faith and in obedience to the prompting of the Holy Spirit. Ministry gifts also known as the five-fold ministry gifts or offices are placed by the Holy Spirit; not everyone has ministry gifts. God Himself anoints and commissions those who serve in an office for ministry. Motivational gifts are part of a believer's personality; it is through these motivational gifts a believer develops the temperament with which he ministers for the Lord. Each believer has motivational gifts that combine to make up his spiritual personality.

Since this study is only on the office of the prophet; I am not going to define each of the ministry gifts or the motivational gifts; doing so would take us far off of our subject for this study.

Ministry gifts or Offices:

"Christ Himself gave the apostles, the prophets, the evangelists, the pastors and teachers, to equip His people for works of service, so that the body of Christ may be built up." (Ephesians 4:11-12)

There are five ministry gifts or offices in the body of Christ:

1. Apostles

2. Prophets

3. Teachers

4. Evangelists

5. Pastors

Motivational Gifts:

"We have different gifts, according to the grace given to each of us. If your gift is prophesying, then prophesy in accordance with your faith, if it is serving, then serve; if it is teaching, then teach; if it is to encourage, then give encouragement; if it is giving, then give generously; if it is to lead, do it diligently; if it is to show mercy, do it cheerfully." (Romans 12:6-8)

There are seven motivational gifts in the body of Christ:

1. Prophecy

2. Serving

3. Teaching

4. Exhortation

5. Giving

6. Administration

7. Mercy

Manifestation Gifts:

"But to each one is given the manifestation of the Spirit for the common good. For to one is given the word of wisdom through the Spirit, and another the word of knowledge according to the same Spirit; to another faith by the same Spirit, and to another gifts of healing by the one Spirit, and to another the effecting (working) of miracles, and to another prophecy, and to another the distinguishing (discerning) of spirits, to another various kinds of tongues, and to another the interpretation of tongues. But one and the same Spirit works all these things, distributing to each one individually just as He wills." (I Corinthians 12:7-11 NASB)

The manifestation gifts often operate together. A word of prophecy can contain words of knowledge and words of wisdom. An interpretation of a tongue can contain words of knowledge and words of wisdom. The gift of working of miracles and the gifts of healing almost always operate with the gift of faith.

It is important that you be able to distinguish the manifestation gifts of the Holy Spirit in order to recognize which gifts are operating in various situations. These gifts operate whether or not they are recognized and identified. As each gift is discussed examples will be given, and other gifts that are operating at the same time will be pointed out. For this reason, examples may be repeated from time to time under the various categories to demonstrate the different gifts are operating at the same time. This is to help you recognize how these gifts can operate together.

There are nine manifestation gifts of the Holy Spirit and they are broken down into three categories. Following is a list by category and the gifts that belong in each:

Utterance Gifts

1. Gift of Prophecy

2. Gift of Speaking in Tongues

3. Gift of Interpretation of Tongues

Revelation Gifts

1. Gift of a Word of Wisdom

2. Gift of a Word of Knowledge

3. Gift of Discerning of Spirits

Power Gifts

1. Gift of Faith

2. Gift of Working of Miracles

3. Gifts of Healing

For the purposes of this study, we will discuss the manifestation gifts by category. The order is not really significant. I have chosen to discuss the utterance gifts first simply because these are the most visible in churches today. The best gift and the most important gift is the one needed for the occasion.

To help everyone better understand how the various categories of gifts operate together I have chosen to discuss how these categories of gifts operate in my life. I operate through one of the five-fold ministry gifts, in the office of a prophet. All of the manifestation gifts have operated at one time or another in my ministry. As you go through this study, I will be discussing various ways the Lord has operated the manifestation gifts in my life.

The Lord does not give a Spirit-filled believer just one manifestation gift; all are available to be used when the occasion arises. There are some who feel more comfortable operating through a single gift, but again, all the manifestation gifts are resident once the believer has been infused with the power of the Holy Spirit. The Lord directs how the manifestation gifts operate. The motivation gifts that operate within me are mercy, exhortation, and giving. By far, the principal motivational gift through which I operate is mercy with exhortation running a close second. Giving motivates me as well, but since I am not a wealthy person my giving is limited to times when the Lord prompts me to give. Life experience has taught that you cannot out give God. It is a blessing to be able to meet someone's needs.

Questions for Study and Discussion

1. Which of the manifestation gifts of the Holy Spirit does the prophet use as tools to operate effectively in the office of the prophet?

2. Is everyone who operates through the manifestation gifts of the Holy Spirit a prophet? Please explain.

3. Are the manifestation gifts only for public operation? Please explain.

4. When do the manifestation gifts become resident within the believer?

5. When the Holy Spirit calls a believer to operate through one of the manifestation gifts there may be a physical response. Please explain.

6. Is it appropriate to operate through the manifestation gifts in a service where they are not welcome to operate? Please explain.

7. Who is in charge of a service when it comes to operating through the manifestation gifts of the Holy Spirit?

8. Believers who minister through the manifestation gifts of the Holy Spirit need to do what before ministering.

9. The Holy Spirit imparts three categories of gifts upon believers. List the categories and list the gifts that belong to each category.

CHAPTER 8

UTTERANCE GIFTS

The Gift of Prophecy

Prophecy is speaking under the inspiration of the Holy Spirit words imparted from the mind of God to His chosen mouthpiece. These are not words from the believer's own thoughts, but words that come from God.

Scripture defines the gift of prophecy further by saying, "But he that prophesies, speaks unto men to edification, and exhortation, and comfort." (I Corinthians 14:3, KJV)

There are only two places in the Word of God that encourage believers to covet anything, and they are both found in I Corinthians. The first, "But covet earnestly the best gifts." (I Corinthians 12:31, KJV) The second, "Wherefore, brethren, covet to prophesy, and forbid not to speak with tongues." (I Corinthians 14:39, KJV)

The manifestation gift of prophecy is different from the office of a prophet. The office of the prophet is one of the five-fold ministry gifts or offices. We will spend considerable time discussing the difference between the gift of prophecy and the office of the prophet in this study. Prophets operate through this gift, but prophecy spoken by a prophet will be quite different. When a prophet speaks a word of prophecy, it will often contain revelation.

Some have questioned if a word of prophecy can be written down and read. The answer to that question is yes. A message can also be presented as the Lord speaks to the believer, and then written down. Messages given in a gathering of believers are not given from memory, at least that is not how the Lord operates when I receive words from the Lord. Often the Lord speaks the words to me, and I simply repeat what I am hearing to the body of Christ. Other times, it is as if the Holy Spirit etches the words in my mind, and I read them as if they were written on a paper.

Several times in scripture prophets wrote down messages, the Lord had given. In Exodus the scripture says, "When Moses went and told the people all the Lord's words, and laws, they responded with one voice, 'Everything the Lord has said we will do.' Moses then wrote down everything the Lord had said." (Exodus 24:3) From this scripture you learn that Moses wrote down what the Lord said after the prophet had given the word to the people. He did this so there would be a written record.

In Jeremiah 36:32, the prophet received a word from the Holy Spirit that he then dictated to the scribe Baruch. The scribe not only wrote the word down, Jeremiah had Baruch take it to the king and read it to him. If it was acceptable to do this in Bible times, I believe it is acceptable in this present day. I suggest that you not read a word from the Lord if you are not a good reader. If your prophecy includes names from scripture, know how to pronounce them before you attempt to give that word in public.

Another example of the Lord directing a prophet to write a message is found in Habakkuk 2:2. "Then the Lord replied: 'Write down the revelation and make it plain on tablets so that a herald may run with it." In this scripture God directed Habakkuk to right down a message and have a runner take the message to other places and deliver that same word multiple times.

In Revelation, John was instructed to, "Write on a scroll what you see and send it to the seven churches: to Ephesus, Smyrna, Pergamum, Thyatira, Sardis, Philadelphia and Laodicea." (Revelation 1:11) Understand this was instruction given to John concerning the revelation he was receiving from the Holy Spirit. He sent that revelation along with a personalized word of prophecy to each church.

Many of the letters contained in the New Testament were filled with simple prophecy to edify, encourage, and comfort the churches. The instruction was to make sure the letters were read in other nearby churches.

These are just a few of the times where a prophet was instructed by God to write the message, there are many other examples. As you read the scripture, I challenge you to identify more of these situations. Especially when revelation is given, the method of presentation is not as relevant as the words that are read or spoken under the anointing of the Holy Spirit.

When I first started receiving prophecy from the Holy Spirit, I would write it down and pray over it. I often received the message in parts. As I prayed about what I received the Lord would expand it until I had received the full message. As I have matured, my faith has developed to the point I simply speak what I am hearing Him say. When a message is written out and read, be flexible and open for the Lord to change that message as it is being given. Remember we speak by faith out of obedience.

For those who operate through the gift of prophecy, I challenge you write down what you are hearing and pray over it. Ask the Lord to anoint the message you have received and direct how He wants those words to be handled. Prophecy can come from the Holy Spirit just for the believer simply to express the Lord's love for him and to encourage him. Prophecy can confirm what the Lord is saying or doing through others in a service. It can also be given to build up the body of Christ and to comfort them. For this reason. it is essential to ask the Holy Spirit for His direction when a message is received.

God wants Spirit-filled believers to prophesy. There are some points I want to make about the manifestation gift of prophecy.

Prophecy is given under the impulse or anointing of the Holy Spirit. Prophecy is not given as a sermon; however, a sermon can include prophecy. A prophetic utterance in a service should be short, lasting only a few minutes. Prophecy spoken through a prophet can be longer at times when that prophecy contains revelation.

The manifestation gift of prophecy as defined in I Corinthians 14:3, does not usually include words of wisdom or words of knowledge. Usually, this gift ministers to encourage and to exhort the people of God to live righteous, faithful lives, and to comfort those who are enduring through the trials of life.

The message of prophecy may expose what is in a person's heart. This would be to offer encouragement to those battling depression, those who are anxious or those who have been beaten down. This message would be given to build strength, and to warn against sin that might bring judgment, or to strengthen them in their faith.

The church should not view prophecy as an infallible. Misuse of this gift can include someone who gives a message that is filled with their own human opinions. It could be used by someone who wants to impress others by giving a word that does not come from God. This is why the word of God says all prophecy should be tested. It should promote Godly living and it should be given by someone who is living a godly life. (I Corinthians 12:1-3)

Prophecy is God spoken; no one can truly prophesy unless the Holy Spirit speaks through them. Revelation 19:10 says, "For the testimony (or evidence) of Jesus is the spirit of prophecy."

Prophecy is given to the body of Christ when God Himself initiates a message that is given through someone as prompted by God. (II Peter 1:21)

I have a caution when it comes to what is called, "personal prophecy." Be very careful! I have seen lives adversely affected by a busybody speaking what they say is a word from the Lord for a specific individual. Does God do this? Yes. Has this practice been badly abused? You bet!

God doesn't need our help advising people how they should be living their lives. Christians now days often look at the way someone is living their life and feel it will make a bigger impact when they are giving life advice if they add the words, "Thus says the Lord." Before you approach someone with what you believe is a personal prophecy from God, you better be sure it is His word not yours.

We will suffer consequences from God Himself by putting His name to something that is only our opinion. Let God be God. If someone calls someone out for a special ministry, it better be God not you!

I know of believers who have sold everything they had to their name to go into the mission field after receiving a so-called word from the Lord, when that prophetic word was not from Him. Personal prophecy if from the Lord will be validated first in their own spirit and then through multiple other sources. When God calls someone into ministry of any kind. Everywhere they turn, God will be sending confirmation after confirmation. If you do not witness with a word spoken over you, it is most likely not from the Lord. If you do not receive multiple confirmations from the Lord as you seek Him over a word that has been spoken over you, let it go!

My husband and I were at a charismatic conference many years ago. A woman came up to us and said she had a prophetic word for my husband. He told her to go ahead and give it to him. Now, this was a woman we had never seen before. She did not know anything about me or my husband. She said the Lord had shown her that he needed to lose weight. That was the full word.

The reason I am sharing this is because, this happens too often in the body of Christ. There are people who see someone who has very visible issues, and they attempt to address those issues and attach the Lord's name to whatever they say. People like this have done great damage to fragile people. When God reaches out to someone, He does it in love. When people speak false prophecy, it can crush people who truly need to be cared for. My husband told the woman it was not a word from the Lord, and that she should mind her own business. God is not in the business of embarrassing people.

Examples of prophecy in scripture:

The first time Samuel heard from the Lord, He spoke a prophetic word to Samuel saying, "See, I am about to do something in Israel that will make the ears of everyone who hears about it tingle. At that time, I will carry out against Eli everything I spoke against his family—from beginning to end. For I told him that I would judge his family forever because of the sin he knew about; his sons blasphemed God, and he failed to restrain them. Therefore, I swore to the house of Eli, 'The guilt of Eli's house will never be atoned for by sacrifice or offering.'" (I Samuel 3:11-14) "The Lord was with Samuel as he grew up, and He let none of Samuel's words fall to the ground." (I Samuel 3:19)

This was a prophetic word that contained words of wisdom that came true very quickly after it was spoken. To summarize what happened, Eli's sons died in battle and when Eli heard about it, he fell off the chair he was sitting on and broke his neck and died.

In Luke 1:5-38, The Lord sent the angel Gabriel to give a prophetic word to Zacharias when he went into the Holy of Holies to minister before the Lord in his capacity as high priest. Gabriel told Zacharias that his prayers had been heard and that his wife Elizabeth was going to have a son who was to be called John. He went on to say that the child would be a joy and delight to him and many would rejoice because of his birth. He also told Zacharias that the child would be great in the sight of the Lord. This child that was foretold became John the Baptist. This message from God delivered through the angel Gabriel included prophecy, a word of knowledge and a word of wisdom.

When Elizabeth was in her 6th month of pregnancy, God sent the angel Gabriel to Mary telling her that the Lord had chosen her to conceive and bring forth a son who would be called the Son of God. The word that Gabriel spoke was a word of prophecy that contained words of wisdom.

The Gifts of Tongues and Interpretation

Because the gift of speaking in tongues must operate together with the gift of interpretation of tongues for public ministry, they have been combined for this study. These are the only two manifestation gifts of the Holy Spirit that were not in operation in the Old Testament.

The gift of speaking in tongues is simply speaking a message in a language unknown to the believer under the supernatural power of the Holy Spirit. This could be a language that is spoken somewhere else in the world, or it can be a heavenly language.

There are two ways the Holy Spirit manifests the gift of speaking in tongues. The first is through a devotional language for private edification and it needs no interpretation. This is referred to as a prayer language. "For anyone who speaks in a tongue does not speak to people, but to God. Indeed, no one understands them; they utter mysteries by the Spirit." (I Corinthians 14:2)

When the Holy Spirit calls a believer to intercessory prayer, tongues can be used to do battle in the spiritual realm on behalf of one or more of God's people who are in desperate need. This is one of the greatest benefits of the gift of speaking in tongues.

"And in the same way the Spirit also helps our weakness. We do not know what we ought to pray for, but the Spirit Himself intercedes for us through wordless groans. And He who searches our hearts knows the mind of the Spirit, because the Spirit intercedes for God's people in accordance with the will of God." (Romans 8:26-27)

It is important that you respond when the Lord calls you to intercede for others who are in need. As you are obedient, the Holy Spirit will trust you more and more. There may be times you will not know why you are praying for the person that the Lord laid upon your heart to pray for, and you may never know the outcome. Obedience is required when the burden to pray comes upon you.

The Holy Spirit has called me to intercede on behalf of myself and my family multiple times throughout our 46 years of marriage. When I was in labor with our first son, there were complications and my son's heartbeat was lost. I began to intercede for my child and myself immediately upon recognizing there were problems. This was not one of those times I received a burden to pray from the Holy Spirit. I simply knew there were problems, and I knew the Holy Spirit could resolve them. When it was determined that if the baby was to survive, an emergency Cesarean section needed to be performed, I prayed urgently in the Spirit.

Before they administered the anesthetic, I was praying in the Spirit. When I awoke in the recovery room, I was told that I had a healthy baby boy. The doctors sent my husband home. He took the phone off the hook, and went to bed. This was reasonable for someone who had been at the hospital throughout the entire 29-1/2 hours of labor, and the surgery that brought our son into the world.

Not long after my husband left the hospital, I developed a pounding headache and I advised the nurse. She took my blood pressure, and all at once she started barking orders, all of which had the term "STAT" attached to them. I overheard the nurse say I was hemorrhaging and going into shock. The hospital at this point tried and failed to get my husband on the phone. They called his father who was next on the contact list. His dad drove across town to our house to get my husband out of bed and over to the hospital. As I was slipping in and out of consciousness, I became aware that I was praying in tongues. When I finally became stable, I was in the intensive care unit in critical condition receiving the first of two blood transfusions. It was an act of the Holy Spirit that spared my life that day, and I believe that those prayers I was offering in tongues were instrumental in moving God's hand.

The Holy Spirit often calls me to times of intercession; sometimes these calls come by the Holy Spirit waking me up in the middle of the night. I have been awakened to a vision of a face of a woman screaming and crying. I instantly knew it was the Holy Spirit calling me to pray. It is difficult to pray in situations like this because I don't know the person or what is wrong. I just know to pray, and the Holy Spirit knows best how to pray through me. I have learned when I am obedient to the Holy Spirit to pray in situations like this my prayers might be the reason that person survives.

I have also been awakened in the night to a vision of a lost desperate looking child. I did not know the child, but I knew the Lord was calling me to pray. I prayed in the Spirit until the burden to pray lifted, and I went back to sleep. When I awoke in the morning, the Spirit had refreshed me as if I had slept the entire night.

One time, the Holy Spirit spoke the name of a person into my spirit and placed a burden upon me to pray for him. I did not know this man and had never heard his very unusual name before. I prayed over a several week period for this man. One night I was watching the evening news, and I heard this man's name. I perked up to listen. They were announcing that this man had just been named to a very high cabinet position by the president of the United States. Now, I don't know why the Holy Spirit placed this burden upon me; I just know that He called me to pray. In this case He rolled back the curtain to show me the circumstances surrounding this call to pray. My prayer could have been for the president who was trying to choose between the various candidates. It could also have been for the man himself who was praying about whether he should accept the position that had been offered. I will never know.

The second way the gift of speaking in tongues operates is through public manifestation, and this always requires interpretation. "If anyone speaks in a tongue, two or at the most three should speak, one at a time, and someone must interpret. If there is no interpreter the speaker should keep quiet in the church and speak to himself and to God." (I Corinthians 14:27-28)

The public operation of the gift of tongues can be expressed in three different ways in a public setting.

1. The most common way this gift operates is through a message given in tongues followed by the interpretation.

2. Tongues can also operate through a public prayer. This type of prayer needs to be interpreted so that those present can understand the prayer and agree.

3. The third way the gift of tongues can function in public is through a song in tongues with the interpretation being given in song.

The proof text for all three of these expressions is found in I Corinthians 14:13-16. "For this reason, the one who speaks in a tongue should pray that they may interpret what they say. For if I pray in a tongue, my spirit prays, but my mind is unfruitful. So, what shall I do? I will pray with my spirit, but I will also pray with my understanding; I will sing with my spirit, but I will also sing with my understanding. Otherwise, when you are praising God in the Spirit, how can someone else, who is now put in the position of an inquirer, say 'Amen' to your thanksgiving, since they do not know what you are saying?"

There are no examples of messages in tongues being given throughout the New Testament after the initial infilling of the Holy Spirit was given in Acts, Chapter 2. There are, however, instructions given in I Corinthians 14:5-6, and verse 13, on how the gift of tongues should operate in a public meeting. It says: "I should like every one of you to speak in tongues, but I would rather have you prophesy. The one who prophesies is greater than the one who speaks in tongues, unless someone interprets, so that the church may be edified…For this reason the one who speaks in a tongue should pray that they may interpret what they say."

It is never acceptable to speak a message in tongues in a service unless the interpretation is given. One of the best ways to ensure that the interpretation is available is for the one who gives the message to ask the Holy Spirit for the interpretation. The Holy Spirit imparts the interpretation to one or more people in a service. However, people are not always obedient to the Holy Spirit. Since it is required that messages in tongues be interpreted, if the person who has the anointing to give the interpretation is not obedient, you will be able to tell the body what the Spirit is saying. Having the interpretation also gives you the ability to confirm that the interpretation is accurate. You may never have to give the interpretation, but you need to have the interpretation in case it is needed.

If someone interprets the word, but the interpretation the speaker received is different from what was spoken as the interpretation, then the one who spoke the message in tongues should give the interpretation they received. It may be that the other person who spoke was giving a separate prophecy. These things can happen when people are just learning to minister.

Each time the Lord has called upon me to speak messages in tongues, the Holy Spirit has provided a new language, different from my prayer language. When this happens, it is just one more confirmation that it is the Holy Spirit speaking. Usually, when the Lord places a burden upon me to intercede for someone or some situation, He gives a different language for this purpose as well.

There may be times the one being called to pray will not know why they are praying for the person that the Lord laid upon their heart for prayer, and they may never know the outcome. We need to obey when the Lord calls us to pray.

Questions for Study and Discussion

1. Define Prophecy.

2. According to I Corinthians 14:3, why is prophecy given?

3. What is the difference between the gift of prophecy and the office of the prophet?

4. When a word of prophecy is received how should that word be handled?

5. Define the gift of speaking in tongues and the gift of interpretation of tongues.

6. The gift of speaking in tongues operates in two ways. What are they?

7. When a message in tongues operates in public what is required?

8. A message in tongues given in public can be expressed in different ways. What are they?

CHAPTER 9

REVELATION GIFTS

The Gift of a Word of Wisdom

The gift of a word of wisdom is a supernatural revelation by the Holy Spirit that comes from the mind of God revealing His plans and purposes. This revelation is usually only a small piece of information. The revelation can be concerning a specific situation or it may answer a question. The revelation can give insight and understanding into a specific word of knowledge. This gift always speaks concerning the future.

People often refer to this gift as the gift of wisdom, but that is inaccurate. There is no gift of wisdom. It is the gift of a word of wisdom. God gives every believer His wisdom, as they learn more and more who He is, and they begin to recognize Him interacting with them. As the believer reads the Word and studies what they are reading, the wisdom of God is imparted to them. Praise and worship can allow the Lord to impart His wisdom into a believer. Simply waiting on the Lord and listening for His voice will also allow the Lord to impart godly wisdom within the believer. The gift of a word of wisdom operates within a believer to supernaturally warn or prepare God's people about things that are going to happen in the future.

This gift often operates together with the gift of prophecy and the gift of a word of knowledge. Though, it is not restricted to operating with any other gift. The Holy Spirit does not impart large amounts of wisdom concerning the future. Receiving words of wisdom, does not mean that a believer knows everything that is going to happen in the future. That would be overwhelming!

Words of wisdom can be conditional or unconditional. When a word of wisdom is conditional, prayer can change the outcome. Many times, certain criteria must be met for a word of wisdom to take place. When an unconditional word of wisdom is given, no amount of prayer will change the outcome.

A word of wisdom is not always for public operation. There are times these words are given by the Holy Spirit to reveal something about which the believer is to pray and intercede.

Some examples of the gift of a word of wisdom being given in scripture include the following:

God revealed the coming of the flood to Noah through the gift of a word of wisdom, in Genesis 6. Along with the revelation, God gave Noah specific instructions to follow so that life could be preserved. This was an unconditional word of wisdom.

In Genesis 18, God sent three angels to Abraham with a word of wisdom that He was going to destroy the cities of Sodom and Gomorrah because of their wickedness. This was a conditional word of wisdom. If just ten righteous men had been found, the cities would have been spared.

King Hezekiah, in II Kings 20, became sick, and sent for the prophet Isaiah to ask the Lord if he would recover. Initially, the Lord told the prophet that Hezekiah would die from his illness. When Hezekiah heard this, he repented and interceded before the Lord, reminding Him of all that he had done to serve Him. Because Hezekiah humbled himself and prayed, the Lord sent Isaiah back to tell him that He would give him 15 more years of life. Our prayers can change the mind of the Lord.

Jonah was called by the Lord to go to Nineveh, and tell the people that their city was going to be overthrown in 40 days because of their sin. Initially, Jonah ran from God instead of doing what the Lord told him to do. It takes a lot of boldness and a serious lack of godly wisdom to tell the Lord, "No" when He calls you to do something for Him. The Lord convinced Jonah through life circumstances (being eaten by a large fish) that he needed to obey God.

I have heard it said that the people of Nineveh worshipped a fish god. How appropriate to have a fish deliver the prophet calling the people to repent. It must have been an awesome sight for the people of Nineveh to see the prophet of God delivered to them in a pile of fish vomit. I am sure it was equally humbling for Jonah to go through this.

Let's think about this situation for a moment. It is reasonable to believe that fish have to digest what they eat much like human beings do. Digestion in humans occurs when digestive juices (acid) break down the food that has been consumed. After being in the fish for several days, Jonah would have been exposed to the digestive juices in the belly of the fish. His skin might have been bleached white, and perhaps his hair would have been partially or completely dissolved. He might have been without some or all of his clothing at that point.

When Jonah finally obeyed the Lord and went to Nineveh, the message was received, the people repented, and the Lord spared the city of Nineveh. Perhaps, Jonah, had a personal agenda as he proclaimed his message to the city. Maybe that is why he ran from the Lord when he was called upon to preach to Nineveh. He may have believed they deserved to be overthrown because of their sin. When the people of the city repented, the city was spared, and Jonah became angry with God.

There is a lesson for all those who receive messages from the Lord in this account of Jonah. God has not called believers to judge the lost. That is the Lord's job. We are to demonstrate God's love to the lost. Believers are called to lovingly correct believers. This is to be done in private and with humility. Before any believer ventures into the waters of correcting another believer, go to God for His direction. Only if directed by God should you attempt to correct another believer. We are all imperfect. God transforms us in His timing. If you carry sin in your own life, perhaps that is where you need to direct your attention. Pray for the one you are wanting to correct;

God can transform the believer as well as drawing the lost to His truth.

A prophet's responsibility is to hear the word of the Lord, speak as directed, and pray that the word will be received. We are not to hope for someone's downfall. If you study the story of Jonah, the Lord did not take His hand off of him just because he got angry when the Lord spared that city. In the end the Lord ministered to Jonah, restored, and blessed him.

Understand that the word of wisdom Jonah received concerning Nineveh was conditional. By sending Jonah to Nineveh, God was giving the people one last chance to repent before the city was destroyed. The city was spared because the people heard the message of the Lord and repented. Had they not responded to the word, the city would have been overthrown as the message had said.

Jesus foretold the destruction of the temple of Jerusalem in multiple scriptures; these were unconditional words of wisdom. (Matthew 24, Luke 21, and Mark 13)

We read the account of a word of wisdom that was given to Zacharias in Luke 1:11-13. The angel of the Lord appeared to him and told him that Elizabeth was going to have a son and they were to name the child John.

In Luke 1:26-35, Elizabeth was six months pregnant when the angel Gabriel, was sent by God to Nazareth to speak a word of wisdom to a virgin named Mary, telling her that she had been chosen by God to conceive and bring forth His Son, who was to be named Jesus.

Agabus the prophet took Paul's belt and bound his own hands and feet, and gave a word of wisdom to Paul saying that the Jewish leaders would bind him in this same way if he traveled to Jerusalem, in Acts 21:11-33. In reality, it was the Roman soldiers that bound Paul, not the Jewish leaders.

The Holy Spirit uses humans when the manifestation gifts are in operation. We must be careful not to add or read into a word the Lord has given. The message Agabus gave was no less a word of wisdom, regardless of who bound Paul. These are only a few of the recorded words of wisdom listed in the Old and New Testaments.

Many years ago, while sitting in a church service the Lord spoke to me. He gave a revelation through the gift of a word of wisdom telling me that He wanted to heal a specific woman who had been diagnosed with a terminal disease. This woman was 22 years old and a newlywed. The pastor had told the congregation that this young woman had a terminal blood disease.

When I received this word, an argument ensued between God and me. I told the Lord if I gave this word and the young lady died, the leadership of the church would call into question the ministry He had established in me. The Lord responded that He had given me this message and He asked if I was going to be obedient. He explained that it was not my reputation on the line but His. As I was giving the word the Lord gave specific instructions for the leadership of the church to follow. These instructions were that the leadership was to meet with this young lady, and pray over her several times over a period of several weeks. They were to, anoint her in the name of Jesus and pray over her in order for this woman to be healed.

This was a conditional word of revelation from the Lord. The only thing the pastor and leadership heard was that the Lord wanted to heal this young lady. I personally made several appointments to pray over this young lady; but no one, not the pastors nor the elders, not even any of the ladies who were in leadership in that church would get together and pray for this young lady as the Lord had instructed. As time went by, this young lady died. Of course she died! The Lord's instructions had not been followed.

Shortly after the young lady's death, I was approached by the leadership of the church; they said they believed me to be a false prophet. They directed me to meet with them to determine if what was being spoken through me from the pulpit was witchcraft or from the Lord. I was told to remain silent until they determined whether or not I was a false prophet. Not another word was to be spoken to the congregation. I have to tell you this was a very painful time in my ministry. My first inclination was to leave the church. I prayed and asked the Lord to release me from His assignment to that body of believers. God told Me, "No, I needed to stay." He said that He was directing this situation. Any prophet operating in a church must submit to the leadership of that church. If a prophet is told to sit down and be quiet, that is what the prophet is to do.

I agreed to meet with the pastor and the leadership, but I had a condition. If they determined me to be a true prophet of God, I asked that they anoint me and set me apart to that ministry. The pastor agreed.

I spent a great deal of time praying over this situation, I knew what I had spoken came from the Lord. It was hard to forget the argument I had with the Holy Spirit when I received the word. The leadership had not followed the Lord's instructions so that the young lady could be healed.

The Lord took me through the scriptures on prophecy and how it operated in the body of Christ. He taught me about conditional and unconditional words of revelation. He revealed that the leadership of the church had been untruthful with the congregation about the diagnosis given to the young lady. He told me that she had a deadly disease that was transmitted sexually, and the stigma surrounding this disease was the reason the leadership had been untruthful with the congregation. He also revealed that the leadership had ignored the instruction from God because they were afraid if this young lady died it would reflect poorly on them. In essence, they were afraid for their own reputations. I was not instructed to confront the leadership about this, but the Holy Spirit prepared me for the meeting.

The Lord used this situation to teach the leadership of the church about conditional words of wisdom. I am not a Bible scholar as some of those in leadership at this church were. All I could do was say what the Lord had given me to say. He alone would have to do the work.

The week before I was to meet with the leadership, people from the congregation who had received healings and miracles in response to the words the Lord had spoken through me began to call members of the leadership team. They reported how the Lord had worked in their lives. Even some on the leadership team had themselves received healings.

The Lord showed up to defend Himself at the meeting and the leadership was humbled. They allowed me to go through the scriptures explaining to them about conditional words of revelation. I did not accuse anyone of a lack of faith, and I did not confront them about their untruthfulness with the congregation. I did not tell them that the Lord had revealed to me the actual disease that the young lady was battling. I simply explained how conditional words of revelation operated and how prayer can change the outcome. I also emphasized how necessary it was to do what the Lord instructed when a conditional word of revelation was given.

At the end of the meeting, I was told that they were going to consider what had been said, pray about it, and I would be notified by mail. I left the meeting fully expecting the leadership to declare me to be a false prophet and determine that I was actually practicing witchcraft in the church; otherwise, why not simply call me with their decision.

Over the next few weeks, I spent a great deal of time praying and waiting on the Lord. The Lord reassured me that He was at the center of this; but to be honest with you, I was truly lacking faith in the outcome. A month went by and I continued to attend the church. While the Lord continued to speak to me; He did not give any messages for the congregation. He knew I could not speak them. Six weeks after the meeting with the leadership, I received a letter stating that they had determined what was being spoken through me was from the Lord, and they set a date to anoint me as a prophet of God.

The leadership decided to acknowledge before the congregation that the Lord was speaking through me. Further, they invited me to speak whenever I heard from the Lord. I could have left the church, and the Lord might never have spoken again in that church. He might never have spoken through me again if I had left the church. Instead, I endured some serious discomfort but as a result, the Holy Spirit was welcomed in the church. The order of the services was changed allowing those to whom the words applied to receive ministry while the anointing was there.

Understand church leadership is made up of humans; it is never acceptable to give false information to the body of Christ. Leadership and pastors are responsible to God for what takes place in their services. Humans are flawed and can make mistakes. Anyone who ministers through the manifestation gifts or in any other way in the body of Christ, must be willing to be corrected. These leaders were trying to do the right thing in this situation, though they made a mistake in not obeying the word the Lord had given. I don't believe they had a vendetta against me. Going through this time was very difficult; but valuable lessons were learned by all those involved.

The Gift of a Word of Knowledge

The gift of a word of knowledge is a revelation given by the Holy Spirit of a small portion of the knowledge that is in the mind of God. It is a supernatural operation of the Holy Spirit that places this information into the mind of a believer. This is specific information that would not be learned in any other way, and it deals with what has already happened or what is currently taking place. This is not the gift of knowledge. Just as with the gift of a word of wisdom, having all knowledge would be overwhelming. The gift of a word of knowledge is simply a word.

God does not drop large amounts of knowledge into someone's mind about the wrongs a person has committed over a lifetime. A person who operates through this gift does not know all the things that have occurred in a person's life, nor does he know all the wrongs that person may have done. God is not in the business of embarrassing the people who follow him.

The difference between the gift of a word of wisdom and the gift of a word of knowledge is this; the word of wisdom is a revelation concerning the future, and the word of knowledge is revelation concerning past occurrences or things that are happening at the present time.

Revelation can come in several different ways:

1. The Holy Spirit can implant revelation within a believer.

2. Revelation can come through tongues and interpretation or through prophecy.

3. An angel can be used to deliver revelation.

4. Revelation can come through a vision or a dream.

It cannot be emphasized enough that not all words of knowledge are for public ministry. The Holy Spirit often reveals things that are confidential in nature. Just because a believer receives a word of knowledge or a word of wisdom, it doesn't mean the word needs to be shared. Ask the Lord why He has given the revelation. Many times, the Holy Spirit reveals things concerning a person's past, to allow for effective ministry. A word of knowledge might be given just to call the believer to pray concerning the information that has been revealed.

Everyone including myself has things in their background that would be embarrassing if revealed. There are people who have embarrassing illnesses, some have sexually transmitted diseases, perhaps there was adultery in a person's past, or an individual was convicted of a crime. The Holy Spirit can use knowledge like this to get someone's attention allowing the person involved to know it is truly the Lord speaking.

Understand that receiving a word of knowledge about someone's past is not an indicator that forgiveness is required, especially if you are ministering to a believer. If you are in a service ministering to someone and the Lord gives a word of knowledge about something like this, be discrete but do not ignore a word of knowledge.

The Holy Spirit can bring healing, deliverance, or even release from guilt and shame through a word of knowledge about someone's past. When the Holy Spirit gives a word of knowledge like this, be careful; don't to go spreading this around within the church body or anywhere else for that matter. In cases like this speak the word of knowledge only to the individual involved and never mention it again. God will hold you accountable if you dare mention to others what the Lord has revealed to you in private concerning someone's personal issues.

A word of knowledge can be given by the Holy Spirit for a specific individual whose name is revealed, but the message can be spoken to a congregation without using that person's name when the Lord directs. While the word is given for a specific individual there might also be others in the congregation to whom the word applies. By speaking the word to the congregation while the anointing of the Lord is present, others can also receive ministry. For this reason, the one receiving the word of knowledge must seek the counsel of the Holy Spirit to determine how best to present a word of knowledge.

Examples of the gift of a word of knowledge include:

In I Samuel 3:8, it was through a word of knowledge Eli determined Samuel was hearing the voice of the Lord.

A word of knowledge was given to Nathan regarding the affair between King David and Bathsheba, in II Samuel 12:1-14. This word of knowledge operated with the gift of faith, as Nathan approached the king to present the message. Nathan could have been thrown into prison or even executed for being so bold as to go to the king and expose his sin. After all, David had just conspired to have Bathsheba's husband killed in battle.

A word of knowledge was given to Elisha in II Kings 5:20-27, that revealed the deception of his servant after Naaman the leper was healed.

It was a word of knowledge in Luke 2:29-30, revealing to Simeon that Jesus was the Christ, when He was brought to the temple for His circumcision. This man had been looking for Christ because the Lord had given him a word of wisdom telling him he would not die until he had seen Him.

In verse 38 of that same chapter, the prophetess Anna received a word of knowledge confirming that Jesus was the Christ, and she went on to speak words of wisdom concerning all who were looking for redemption in Jerusalem.

The Gift of Discerning of Spirits

The last of the revelation gifts is the gift of discerning of spirits. Many people in the body of Christ call this the gift of discernment. It is properly called the gift of discerning of spirits. Just as with the other manifestation gifts, this gift operates in different ways. The gift of discerning of spirits gives insight into the realm of spirits through the supernatural operation of the Holy Spirit. This gift can reveal evil spirits as well as good spirits. It allows the believer to see spiritual beings and hear actual voices in the spiritual realm. However, one of the primary operations of this gift is to understand a human spirit. In other words, this gift allows the believer through the power of the Holy Spirit to understand what is motivating someone. This gift also reveals the kind of spirit behind a supernatural manifestation. When believers see visions, or hear spiritual voices, it is through the Holy Spirit gift of discerning of spirits.

The gift of discerning of spirits operates in the background of all the other gifts that minister through me. Not everyone has the gift of discerning of spirits active in the background of all they do through the Spirit. As a prophet of God this gift is extremely important to me.

Scripture says, "Watch out for false prophets. They come to you in sheep's clothing, but inwardly they are ferocious wolves. By their fruit you will recognize them…Many will say to me on that day, Lord, Lord did we not prophesy in your name, and in your name drive out demons and, in your name, perform many miracles? Then I will tell them plainly, I never knew you, away from Me, you evildoers!" (Matthew 7:15-23) This scripture is referring to people who minister in the name of the Lord, but who are ministering out of wrong motives.

Understand, God is referring to people who actually prophesy, drive out demons, and perform miracles. The ways these people are ministering is effective. Miraculous things are being done through them. They are saying and doing things that seem to be very holy, but they are not giving God the glory; instead, they are accepting God's glory for themselves. They are operating with wrong motives.

It might surprise you to know that not all people who attend church today do it to get closer to God. There are some who want to get closer to God, but they also have other motives. There are business people, some of whom attend church looking for a pool of people from whom they can financially benefit. There are sexual predators who attend church looking for their next victim. Satan often sends individuals into churches to disrupt the church. One of the ways they do this is by creating opposition to the leadership of the church, attempting to bring the church down from the inside. Often these individuals will go after a pastor, prophet, or others in leadership using sexual enticement that may not be recognized without the gift of discerning of spirits in operation. Some of these individuals will work their way into leadership in the church to undermine what the Holy Spirit of God is doing. It is through the gift of discerning of spirits that leadership, pastors, and prophets will become aware of the traps the devil has set for the church, and they will be able to bind satan and break his power in these situations. The gift of discerning of spirits is indispensable in determining what is motivating someone.

This gift is not given to permit a believer to supernaturally uncover human failings. We already have plenty of people in the body of Christ with that gift, and it is not from the Holy Spirit.

Many times, the Holy Spirit will operate through this gift in order to assist believers in praying and interceding against the powers of darkness. It can also aid in praying more effectively for direction or healing.

Another significant operation of this gift is in ministering deliverance to those bound by the enemy. Acts 16:17, records an account of a woman possessed with a spirit of divination. Paul determined that she was speaking under the influence of an evil spirit, even though what she was saying sounded holy, and he commanded the spirit to leave her.

Demonstrations of the gift of discerning of spirits:

The gift of discerning of spirits was operating when God passed by Moses in Exodus 33:21-23, allowing him to see God's back and hear His voice.

It was through this gift that Samuel was able to hear the voice of the Lord. (I Samuel 3:8) A word of knowledge was given to Eli allowing him to know the Lord was speaking to Samuel, and he was able to instruct Samuel how he should respond to the Lord's voice. (I Samuel 3:9) What Samuel heard was a word of wisdom, but actually hearing the Lord's voice was the gift of discerning of spirits.

When the King of Aram sent his soldiers to take Elisha captive, the gift of discerning of spirits was operating permitting Elisha to see the mountain was full of horses and chariots of fire. Elisha essentially asked the Lord to extend this gift to his servant allowing him to see and not be afraid. (II Kings 6:8-17)

You can read about the transfiguration of Christ in Matthew 17:1-5. "After six days Jesus took with Him Peter, James, and John the brother of James, and led them up a high mountain by themselves. There He was transfigured before them. His face shone like the sun, and His clothes became as white as the light. Just then there appeared before them Moses and Elijah, talking with Jesus." This was a demonstration of the gift of discerning of spirits.

The gift of discerning of spirits was operating when Zacharias was able to see the angel standing on the right side of the altar of incense in Luke 1:11-13. It was through this gift that he was able to see and hear the angel speaking to him concerning Elizabeth having a baby. The angel spoke words of wisdom, but seeing the angel and hearing him were both demonstrations of the gift of discerning of spirits. The fact that the Lord closed Zacharias's mouth until the child was born was the gift of working of miracles in operation.

Later in that same chapter it was the gift of discerning of spirits operating that allowed Mary to see Gabriel and hear him when he came with a word of wisdom telling her that she had been chosen by God to be the mother of His son.

Peter, in Acts 5:1-11, used this gift to determine that Ananias and Sapphira had joined together and lied about the price they had received for the property they sold. Now, there was no sin in trying to keep some of the money, but they lied to the Holy Spirit (God who knows all) about how much they received. These lies cost both of them their lives. Understand Peter had nothing to do with the deaths of Ananias and Sapphira. However, the Holy Spirit through the gift of discerning of spirits revealed their sin to Peter. This scripture is a great demonstration of what can happen when someone tries to deceive the Holy Spirit.

In Acts 8:18-24, the gift of discerning of spirits was used to detect the deception of Simon the sorcerer.

I said earlier in this study that this gift operates in the background of most any ministry that I do for the Lord. This gift has also operated more directly in my life on and off for many years. I was attending a conference in South Carolina with the ladies from my church. When the service started, I became aware of a lesbian spirit around me. I began praying in the Spirit and binding the devil. I also looked to see if I could locate who was being tormented by this spirit. I did this hoping to be able to minister directly to whoever it was. The Lord never revealed who was battling this spirit, but as the service proceeded, I continued to bind that spirit until it lifted. Often times the gift of discerning of spirits will allow for intercession and release from bondage even though you do not know who you are praying for.

I have seen angels and heard them speak. I have also heard the Lord Himself speak to me. It was through the gift of discerning of spirits that I saw the Lord turn His back to me. This happened through a vision I saw while I was engaging in something very sinful. Let me say when you see the Lord turn away, you know you have truly hurt and angered him.

This occurred after I had been saved, received the baptism of the Holy Spirit, and had been appointed by God to operate in the office of a prophet. I was young in my ministry, but I got involved in some things that were very displeasing to the Lord. It was at a time when everything in my life seemed to be crashing down around me. I was in a state of confusion and I gave in to temptation. When I began to participate in what I knew was sin, I saw this vision of the Lord turning away from me. I was crushed! I fell to my knees in front of those I was with and I began to repent. Their response to my doing this was to say simply, "What's the big deal. You can always repent tomorrow." A sense of guilt and shame came over me as I recognized that I had rebelled against my Lord. Repenting did not resolve my problem. I repented and repented but did not feel that the Lord had answered, and I never saw Him turn back toward me.

The Lord continued to operate through me during this time. I would remind you of the scripture that says, "For God's gifts and His call (or commission) are irrevocable." (Romans 11:29) The Holy Spirit continued to give me words for the body of Christ, and as God's spokesman, I had to be obedient to speak the messages He gave me. I was not sensing the power of the Spirit in my life as I had in the past. In fact, each time I received a message from the Lord for the body of Christ, I struggled. I would hear satan reminding me of the terrible things I had done. He would speak to me even as the Lord was speaking. He would say, "Who do you think you are? You can't minister for the Lord. I know who you are and what you have done." I knew that I needed to be obedient to the Lord, but I really felt unworthy and unqualified. I simply could not get release for my sin.

After six years of dealing with the guilt and shame of what I had done, the Lord asked how long I was going to keep repenting for the sin He had already forgiven. I asked the Lord why I had not seen Him turn back toward me. He said that He had forgiven me the first time I had asked, and that He had never abandoned me. He turned from me for a short time because He could not look upon my sin. At that time, He lifted the guilt and shame from me. I had allowed satan to torment me, keeping me in bondage for all those years because I had not forgiven myself. This was what it took for me to get free from the guilt and shame of my past. God quickly forgives us when we truly repent. We are much harder on ourselves than is our precious Heavenly Father. The Lord wants all of His people to be released from the bondage of their past. Perhaps the beginning of that release requires us to forgive ourselves for our own self-sabotage.

Questions for Study and Discussion

1. Define the gift of a word of wisdom.

2. There are two types of words of wisdom. What are they?

3. What is the difference between the two types of words of wisdom?

4. Are all words of wisdom for public operation?

5. Define the gift of a word of knowledge.

6. Does a person who operates through the gift of a word of knowledge know about everything that has happened in a person's life?

7. What is the difference between the gift of a word of wisdom and the gift of a word of knowledge?

8. What are some of the ways revelation is given?

9. Are all words of knowledge for public operation?

10. Define the gift of discerning of spirits.

CHAPTER 10

POWER GIFTS

There are several types of faith listed in scripture. The first is saving faith, "Believe (have faith) in the Lord Jesus Christ and you will be saved." (Acts 16:31)

God gives every human being the faith to believe in the Lord Jesus Christ. Scripture tells us in Titus 2:11-12. "For the grace of God that brings salvation has appeared to all men. It teaches us to say, 'No' to ungodliness and worldly passions, and to live self-controlled, upright and godly lives in this present age."

Proverbs 15:29 says, "The Lord is far from the wicked, but He hears the prayer of the righteous." The only prayer that God promises to answer for the unbeliever is the prayer of salvation.

Hebrews 11:6 says, "And without faith it is impossible to please God, because anyone who comes to Him must believe (or have faith) that He exists and that He rewards those who earnestly seek Him."

The second kind of faith is the fruit of the spirit, "But the fruit of the Spirit is love, joy, peace, patience (longsuffering), gentleness, goodness, faith, meekness, temperance (self-control): against such there is no law." (Galatians 5:22-23, KJV)

This type of faith is developed through life experiences and seeing prayers answered over time. Our growth in the fruit of faith depends on us. We must have a consistent walk with Jesus; we must read the Word of God regularly; and, we must fellowship with the Holy Spirit. In other words, the fruit of faith must be cultivated.

The source of faith within the believer is God the Father, God the Son, and God the Holy Spirit. Faith originates in the Godhead, not the body of Christ. Hebrews 12:2 says, "God is the author and finisher of our faith." Faith does not originate in the heart of man; the Apostle Paul wrote in Romans 10:17, "So then faith cometh by hearing, and hearing by the Word of God." (KJV) The main source of faith comes when someone speaks the true Word of God and it is heard by others.

When we spend time in His presence it produces faith. It is not something we can muster up within ourselves. It must be planted through hearing the Word of God.

It must be nourished through studying and meditating on the Word of God. This allows the Holy Spirit to give us understanding.

Mark 11:22-23 says, "Have faith in God," Jesus answered. "Truly I tell you, if anyone (who believes in the Lord Jesus and follows His commands) says to this mountain, 'Go throw yourself into the sea,' and does not doubt in their heart, but believes that what they say will happen, it will be done for them."

Faith is also a part of the armor of God. Ephesians 6:16 says, "In addition to all this, take up the shield of faith with which you can extinguish all the flaming arrows of the evil one."

Gift of Faith

I Corinthians 12:9 includes faith as one of the nine manifestation gifts of the Holy Spirit. The manifestation gift of faith is supernatural faith that goes beyond human faith. This faith is spontaneously implanted by the Holy Spirit. This kind of faith often kicks in when a believer has come to the end of their own faith. Since it is faith given by the Holy Spirit no action is required to make it operate. This gift is given so that the believer can receive answers to prayer that are often imparted through the gift of working of miracles and or the gifts of healing.

Demonstrations of the gift of faith:

Some of these examples have already been used with other manifestation gifts. It is important that we learn how these gifts operate with other manifestation gifts.

God, through a word of wisdom, revealed the coming of the flood to Noah. (Genesis 6) It was through the operation of the gift of faith, Noah was able to believe for 120 years that the Lord was going to do what He said He would do.

Let's discuss Noah for a few minutes. He was about 500 years old when the Lord spoke to him. He was married and had children. Do you think Noah's wife was able to stand around for 120 years watching her husband build that ark without questioning his sanity or chastising him for all the time and resources he was wasting to build a boat in the middle of the desert? How about his kids? They were probably fully grown when Noah began building the ark. Do you think they escaped the sarcastic comments by others in the city? They were probably the source of many jokes as everyone in the city watched the crazy old man building a boat in the desert! Honestly, I suspect Noah's sons were recruited to help with this construction project.

It was the gift of faith, the gift of a word of wisdom, and the gift of working of miracles operating together that allowed David to be victorious over the giant Goliath in I Samuel 17.

The gift of faith was operating when Elijah gave the word of wisdom to King Ahab that there would not be rain in the land except at his word. (I Kings 17:1-6) This resulted in a drought that lasted three years. The gift of working of miracles operated here because what happened went against the laws of nature.

Elijah called all the prophets of Baal together in I Kings 18:22-40, in order to demonstrate the real God and His power. It was the gift of faith operating in conjunction with the gift of working of miracles that caused God to send fire to ignite the sacrifice and devour it along with the altar itself even though it had been drenched with water. Yet again, Elijah's actions violated the laws of nature.

Daniel, Chapter 1, demonstrates the gift of faith through the actions of the royal family of Israel (Daniel, Shadrach, Meshach and Abednego) when they were captured and enslaved by King Nebuchadnezzar. They chose to remain pure eating only vegetables and drinking water instead of partaking in the royal provision of choice food, meat, and wine. God gave them supernatural faith to believe the king's official would see they were healthier and stronger than any of the other servants of the king even though they were keeping themselves pure.

The Holy Spirit gift of faith can be seen when King Nebuchadnezzar made a golden image and required all the people in the nation to bow and worship it. (Daniel, Chapter 3) Shadrach, Meshach and Abednego stood before the crowd and refused to worship the golden image though ordered to do so under penalty of being thrown into a furnace of fire. Their response to the king was, "If we are thrown into the blazing furnace, the God we serve is able to deliver us from it, and He will deliver us from Your Majesty's hand. But even if He does not, we want you to know, Your Majesty that we will not serve your gods or worship the image of gold you have set up." (Daniel 3:17-18)

When Daniel continued to pray publicly knowing that the king had banned prayer to any god but his, also demonstrated the Holy Spirit gift of faith. When Daniel was cast into the lion's den, he had supernatural faith to believe the Lord would deliver him. (Daniel 6:16-28)

In these cases concerning Daniel, Shadrach, Meshach, and Abednego, the Holy Spirit gift of faith operated to allow a miracle to be received. With Shadrach, Meshach and Abednego, the appearance of a fourth person in the furnace, truly got King Nebuchadnezzar's attention. He was astonished and remarked the fourth person looked like the son of a god. Recognize that when the Lord does a miracle, He works wondrously. The ropes that bound Shadrach, Meshach, and Abednego were burned away; but their clothing was not burned. Not one of them was burned, and there was no smell of smoke on them. Praise God! I encourage you to study Daniel 3 where this account is recorded.

When Jesus was asleep in the boat in Mark 4:35-41, and the storm came up, the disciples thought they would be killed; Jesus simply spoke to the storm. It was the gift of faith that brought about the working of miracles that calmed the storm.

The gift of faith was operating allowing Peter to sleep soundly in prison as the authorities were contemplating putting him to death in Acts 12:6-11. The angel that the Lord sent to free Peter from prison had to shake him to awaken him from his sleep. It was through the gift of discerning of spirits, that Peter was able to see and hear the angel. It was the gift of working of miracles in operation, that allowed the angel to open the prison door and to release the chains that bound Peter.

Gift of Working of Miracles

The gift of working of miracles brings the supernatural power of the Holy Spirit into a situation to change it in a miraculous way. The Holy Spirit can alter or suspend the laws of nature, physics, and science. It is different from the gifts of healing in that these are wonders that do not have to do with healing.

Demonstrations of the gift of working of miracles:

A good demonstration of the gift of the working of miracles is the parting of the red sea in Exodus 14:21-22. The gift of faith was also in operation providing Moses overwhelming expectation to receive this miracle.

The Lord caused a donkey to speak to Balaam in Numbers 22:10-34. The donkey was still a donkey, and anyone tempted to be filled with pride because of the use of any of the manifestation gifts in his life needs to remember the Lord ministers through willing and yielded vessels no matter who or what they are.

Joshua 10:12-14, demonstrates how Joshua through the working of miracles caused the sun and moon to stand still. This supernatural work went against the laws of nature.

The prophet Isaiah in II Kings 20:11, made the shadow on the stairs go back ten steps. This resulted in time actually reversing itself, when Hezekiah asked him for a sign that what the Lord said would come to pass.

It was through the gift of working of miracles that Elisha raised the Shunammite woman's son from the dead. The Lord did not give a word of knowledge to Elisha to tell him what was wrong. The Shunammite woman went hunting for Elisha and when she found him, she had to tell him what was wrong. Even though it had been many days since the boy had died, the gift of faith coupled with the gift of working of miracles operated to raise the child from the dead. (II Kings 4:8-37)

In the Book of Daniel, the gift of working of miracles is demonstrated multiple times as we see the Lord giving Daniel, Shadrach, Meshach and Abednego the supernatural faith to defy King Nebuchadnezzar. Daniel, when he refused to stop praying to the Lord God, was delivered from the lion's den, and Shadrach, Meshach, and Abednego were delivered from the blazing furnace when they refused to worship the golden image Nebuchadnezzar had built.

Notice that the Holy Spirit gift of faith operated bringing supernatural faith into these situations allowing the Holy Spirit gift of working of miracles to be received. What a powerful demonstration of these two gifts of the Holy Spirit! The two gifts operated together to show that the Lord God moves on behalf of those who stand in faith with him!

When Jesus and Peter walked on water in Matthew 14:25-33, it was through the gift of working of miracles. It was a miracle because this action went against the laws of nature. Though many might think the Holy Spirit gift of faith was operating allowing Peter to walk on the water, I suggest it was the fruit of faith instead. Why do I say it was fruit, and not the gift? Because the Holy Spirit gift of faith is supernatural faith given by the Holy Spirit, and it takes no action on behalf of the believer to make it function. If the gift of faith were operating in this situation, Peter would never have sunk into the water. As soon as Peter took his eyes off Jesus, he sunk like a rock.

As I said earlier, the fruit of faith is something that we must cultivate in our lives.

Feeding the multitudes in Matthew 14:15-21, and again in Mark 6:35-44, were both demonstrations of the working of miracles. Of course, the gift of faith was operating in these instances as well.

In John 11:1-44, Jesus raised Lazarus from the dead. This was done through the gift of working of miracles. When attempting to raise someone from the dead, you better have the gift of faith operating in you. Human beings do not possess the type of faith in and of themselves to raise the dead. The gift of faith operates with the gift of working of miracles in these cases.

I must share how the Lord worked miraculously in my family when my husband became disheartened with his work in Georgia. He found a job advertised on the internet for which he was qualified, and he applied. He took a trip to New Mexico to be interviewed for a job at a wastewater treatment plant, and he got the job.

I was working at the time. I had a really good job and didn't want to move. I was praying that the Lord would make it clear to me that this was His will for our family. My husband mailed his acceptance letter back to his new employer and prepared to leave. The day after he sent his acceptance letter, I planned to go into work and tell My supervisor that I was going to have to resign my position. Before I could talk to my boss, the company announced they were closing the Atlanta office, and all employees would be unemployed by the end of April.

No one can tell me the Lord was not in this move. Charlie left for New Mexico in February, 1998. The fact that the company I was working for was closing made me eligible to collect unemployment compensation after the layoff in April. I spent those months selling everything that could be sold and packing for our move. I was supposed to sell the house but that did not happen. I joined my husband in New Mexico in June of 1998 after the boys got out of school for the summer. My husband had already bought a house.

When we moved to New Mexico, the water well at the house we bought went dry only three weeks after we moved in. I have to admit that my attitude was really bad in this situation. After a great deal of whining, anger, and many temper tantrums, I shook my fist at God and asked Him why He had moved us to this dry land where there was no water. I suggest caution if you feel the need to shake your fist at God. He responded by telling me that the spirits of many of the people in this place were as dry as the land itself. He went on to say that there were also many people in this place praying for the water of the Spirit to be poured out upon this dry land. He told me that He had brought me to this place to assist in pointing people to the Lord God. I felt pretty silly after all my temper tantrums to have the Lord tell me that. Yes, I repented. You need to understand that even though God directs your path, it does not mean you will never experience adversity nor will you always immediately understand why the adversity has occurred. Often adversity comes from satan who is trying to get the Lord's people to step away from the call the Lord has on their lives. The adversity we encounter may come from satan; but understand, God can use that adversity to mature us when we call out to Him and humbly lay the adversity at His feet.

Even though the Lord had told me why He brought us to this land, it was still a financial disaster for us! I had been unable to sell our home in Georgia requiring us to pay two mortgage payments each month along with the legal fees involved in suing those who sold us a house with no water. It took a great deal of prayer to forgive those people.

After two and a half years and a great deal of legal negotiations, the insurance companies for the real estate brokers involved, asked us to give them an amount that we would be willing to accept to resolve our water issues. Knowing that there was no guarantee of hitting water if we drilled, we prayed and the Lord impressed upon us to settle for enough money to drill down 1,000 feet, three times searching for water. The insurance companies agreed to our number and told us to expect a check in about ten days.

As my husband and I prayed for a miracle in our situation, the Lord reminded us of a scripture that says in part. "Truly I tell you, if you have faith and do not doubt...you can say to this mountain, 'Go throw yourself into the sea,' and it will be done." (Matthew 21:21) Well, we had a symbolic mountain in front of us.

As we prayed, the Lord directed me to walk around our ten-acre plot of ground several times each day praying and asking Him to move the water under our property to be at the bottom of the hole we were going to drill. Now, I was praying this prayer, but we had no idea at that time where we were going to drill. My husband on the other hand was praying differently. He was asking God where we should drill. For ten days I walked around our property several times a day asking the Lord to move the water. The night before the drillers were to begin drilling, my husband asked God one last time where we should drill. He then went out and stuck a shovel in the ground at the Lord's direction indicating where the workers were to drill.

Ultimately, the Lord provided an underground stream after drilling down only a couple hundred feet. The Lord did a mighty work for us that day, and our well has not stopped running. I thank and praise Him every day for the water He provided. I know the Lord hears and answers prayer. I know that He performs miracles when we pray believing. He has done it for our family many times.

Gifts of Healing

The gifts of healing is the supernatural curing of illnesses, injuries, handicaps, and diseases without the use of natural means. I believe that the Holy Spirit gifts of healing can also supernaturally operate through the skill of a medical professional. Some people may not think that this gift is in operation when it comes to doctors, but I do. The Holy Spirit can use whatever method He desires to bring about a healing.

The doctor can prescribe various medications, but unless the Lord causes those medications to do what they were designed to do, no healing can take place. A surgeon can do what he has been trained to do, but ultimately the Lord God causes the body to respond and to be healed. It is a supernatural manifestation of the Holy Spirit that brings about a healing. These healings can be physical healings; they can also include emotional or even spiritual healings. I have known people who would not go to the doctor because they felt it indicated a lack of faith. I believe God created the medical profession to serve us.

It reminds me of the joke about the man in the flood. He was stuck on the roof of his house as the waters raged around him. He prayed and asked God to save him. A short time later a man in a canoe came along, and asked if he would you like a ride. The man replied no thank you; I have prayed to God, and I am waiting for Him to deliver me. Next a man in a motor boat came along and asked him if he needed a ride? The man replied no thank you; I have prayed to God, and I am waiting for Him to deliver me. Soon a helicopter came along, and the pilot yelled do you need a ride? The man said no thank you; I have prayed to God and I am waiting for Him to deliver me. Finally, the house is swept away and the man drowns. When he gets to heaven, he asks God, why didn't you help me? God said, "I sent you a canoe, a motor boat, and a helicopter!"

The man was so closed minded that he didn't recognize it was God who sent the canoe, the motor boat, and the helicopter. Believers are much the same as the man on the roof. God's people do not recognize His help when He sends it.

When believers pray, they shouldn't tell God how to answer their prayers, and they shouldn't have preconceived ideas of what that answer will look like. Healing can come in many ways; we don't demand God's healing, and it is not for us to tell God how to heal us. We humbly make our needs known to Him, and wait upon Him for His answer.

"And if the Spirit of Him who raised Jesus from the dead is living in you, He who raised Christ from the dead will also give life to your mortal bodies because of His Spirit who lives in you." (Romans 8:11)

Demonstrations of the gifts of healing:

Elisha told Naaman in II Kings 5:4-27, to go and dip seven times in the Jordan River, and he would be healed. In order to receive his healing, Naaman had to be obedient and do what he was told to do.

In Luke you can read the account of the woman who came up to Jesus unannounced and touched the hem of His garment and was instantly healed. This was a demonstration of the gift of faith operating together with the gifts of healing. Jesus exposed her and told her "Daughter, your faith has healed you. Go in peace." (Luke 8:48) Jesus exposed her not to embarrass her but so that she would have nothing to hamper her healing. No one can steal a healing from the mighty God, but the devil might have placed guilt upon the woman for "stealing" a healing that she did not deserve. This can also be a lesson for believers today. Healings are not to be kept undercover. When God performs a healing or miracle in our lives, we need to make it known to others.

Jesus told the lepers to go show themselves to the priests. On the way, they were healed. (Luke 17:12-16)

In John 9:11-33, you find the account where Jesus placed mud on the blind man's eyes and told him to go wash. After having been obedient, he received his healing. Remember the Pharisees and how they interrogated this man trying to find a way to discredit him?

The scripture says in Acts 5:12-15, that Peter was so filled with the power of the Holy Spirit, he was able to heal people by simply walking past them and having his shadow pass over them.

In Acts 19:11-12, healing and deliverance occurred when an apron or handkerchief touched by Paul was taken to a sick person and he touched it. This can also happen today just as it did back then. Understand it is not the apron or the handkerchief that brings healing it is the power of God or the anointing on these items combined with reaching out in faith that brings about the healing.

The Holy Spirit gift of faith has been activated within me to receive healing in my body in many different ways, not the least of which was a healing from seizures when I was 21 years old.

The first time I had a seizure was in my seventh-grade math class. It disrupted the entire class as the teacher tried to deal with me. I did not know what was happening and neither did she. Throughout my junior high and senior high school years and even through business school,

I experienced seizures. The doctors prescribed various medications trying to control the seizures; all they did was dull my senses. Some of those drugs were addictive.

I can't think of anything more humiliating than having a seizure in a classroom full of teenagers. The other students were afraid to be around me. Honestly, I was afraid to be around myself. There were also those students who made fun and treated me like I had some kind of contagious disease. Having medical problems like this can cause very low self-esteem.

I had been anointed and prayed over many times in the evangelical church that I was attending. When you ask the pastor to anoint you and pray for healing and the response is, "I have never done that before, and I can't give you any guarantees." There is little hope of a healing.

A month after my husband and I married, we attended a Charismatic Conference in Pittsburgh, Pennsylvania, where several powerful speakers were teaching on faith and receiving healing. At the end of the week, my husband and I got together and prayed for the Lord to heal me and, Praise God, He did! I don't know all the answers when it comes to healing. I don't know why some people get healed and others do not. I don't know why God heals some parts of a person's body but leaves other issues unresolved. What I do know is that the Lord has touched and healed me many times, and I praise Him for what He has done.

When we prayed to the Lord for healing from these seizures the Holy Spirit gift of faith was activated giving a supernatural faith to receive this healing. As an act of faith, I felt the Holy Spirit was telling me to stop taking my medications. I do not recommend that people stop taking their medications in situations like this, but this was something I felt the Lord wanted me to do. To be safe you should be cleared by a medical professional. By all rights, this decision could have landed me in the hospital in a crisis situation. Many of the medications I was taking were addictive and stopping them might have caused withdrawals. After we prayed, I never had another seizure. Praise the Lord!

Not only did the Lord heal the seizures, but my food allergies and asthma that I was also suffering from were gone as well. There were no withdrawals nor were there any adverse side-affects for not taking the medications. The Lord proved Himself to be faithful.

I have to be honest with you about this. All my food allergies were healed, but I continued to experience seasonal allergies. The asthma was also healed at that time, but about 35 years later I began to experience breathing problems again and had to go back on medication; I praise the Lord for the 35 years during which there were no asthma symptoms.

Instead of acknowledging the healing, my doctor discounted this healing saying that young people often grow out of these kinds of problems. It was very interesting to me that the seizures had stopped and the allergies and asthma went away at exactly the same time my husband and I prayed. I know in my heart God Almighty healed me, and no one can tell me differently.

In most cases where the power gifts are in operation, the gift of faith operates providing supernatural expectation that allows the wonders that take place through the gift of working of miracles or the gifts of healing.

Questions for Study and Discussion

1. List the different types of faith that are referred to in scripture.

2. Define the gift of faith.

3. What is the primary reason the gift of faith is given?

4. Define the gift of working of miracles.

5. Define the gifts of healing.

CHAPTER 11

CHURCH ORDER, PROTOCOLS, AND DISCIPLINE

Each church has its own philosophy and beliefs. They have their own protocols and established order for their services. These are to be respected and followed. Some churches do not believe in; nor do they teach about receiving the Holy Spirit and His manifestation gifts. The Holy Spirit will never anoint someone to minister using these gifts, in a church where they are not recognized. Any believer who attempts to minister these gifts where they are not recognized is operating in the flesh and is out of order. The Holy Spirit does not cause disruption, fear, or confusion. It is possible for a believer to sense the anointing of the Holy Spirit for many reasons. One should never minister these gifts in a service where they are not permitted to operate. You will be out of order.

When the Holy Spirit operates through any of the His gifts in a service, it needs to be done in order so that the flow of the Spirit is not interrupted. I Corinthians 14:39-40 says, "Therefore, my brothers, be eager to prophesy, and do not forbid speaking in tongues. But everything should be done in a fitting and orderly way." Some churches require believers to notify someone in authority if they have a word. This is to assure that any word given is in line with the Word of God.

Another part of ministry protocol is that if visiting another church, and you are not known to the leadership, and/or they do not allow the manifestation gifts to operate in their services, you should not speak. The Holy Spirit will not direct anyone to give a word in a congregation where they are not known.

If the person in charge of the service tells someone to be quiet, that person should stop speaking. If there are questions about why they were told to be quiet, go to that leader after the service to discuss it. If the one in charge of the meeting is out of touch with the Holy Spirit, the Lord will deal with him.

God is not the author of confusion, and when no one takes charge of a service, things can quickly get out of hand. The Lord will honor the obedience of a believer who is asked to stop speaking even if they were operating in the right order, and even if they are not given the opportunity to complete the message. Just obey, be quiet and let the Lord deal with the leader.

When a believer is just starting to minister, they may get so excited about receiving a word that their timing could be wrong. The message may not be for the current service. It may be for a future service. Ask the Lord for direction. God could be speaking a personal word for that believer. God will make it clear if we will ask. Understand that mistakes can happen. The Lord looks at the attitude of your heart when you are ministering in any way. Those who are unwilling to chance making a mistake, and be corrected, may never minister through the manifestation gifts.

When a believer gets a spontaneous word, it does not mean the believer should just interrupt what is already taking place. We must discipline ourself to wait until there is a break in the service. No one should ever minister based on feelings. The Spirit can make Himself known through a physical sense of His presence. This awareness can be very strong, but that does not always mean what you are feeling is an anointing to speak. Enjoy the Lord's presence and wait for His direction.

If the congregation is offering praise and worship through music, you should not try to minister a word over what is taking place. It will interrupt the flow of the Holy Spirit.

God understands and so should we that the Holy Spirit operates in order. If we get ahead of ourself and the person in charge of the service tells us to be quiet, we should stop talking. The leader may recognize us later and let the message come forth; he may not. There is no room for pride when it comes to operating through the manifestation gifts; rather, we should be humble and respectful of the Lord as we minister.

I have been in services where a believer was giving a word from the pulpit while people were going for coffee. When people do that, they are out of order. The Lord will lift His anointing when things like this happen. When someone is giving a message from the Lord, the congregation should give their full attention to what the Lord is saying. Be respectful of the Lord's presence and His anointing.

As a prophet of God, I have been directed by the Holy Spirit to correct a speaker several times. Correction like this is my least favorite part of ministering in the office of the prophet. We don't get to choose which messages we will speak for the Lord. We must obey. As a woman, it is often very difficult for leaders to receive correction from me. You would be amazed at how unteachable leaders can be when they think they have "made it" in their ministry. Often people who have powerful ministries get proud and think they are above correction, especially when it is coming from a woman. If a powerful minister will not receive the correction God sends, He will continue to send that correction until the minister receives it. Often, that means a less gentle method will be used.

When I speak correction, God is the one doing the correcting. I am just the vessel through which He is speaking. Ministers have responded in very disrespectful ways to correction the Lord has spoken through me. I have had leaders ask me who I think I am trying to correct them.

One powerful leader rattled off the list of his very impressive credentials to emphasize how unqualified I was to correct him. If I am willing to speak encouragement to the body, I cannot then refuse to speak correction when directed by God. It is humbling when the Lord directs me to correct someone. It is up to the one being corrected to actually receive the correction the Lord has spoken even through this woman.

If a leader in the body of Christ will not receive correction when God sends someone like me to correct them, they better beware. When a man or woman of God gets off the path the Lord put them on, and they do not receive the correction sent by the Lord, God will get His message across to that leader in another less gentle way. That leader may just find a honking big locomotive headed directly for them. Pastors, evangelists and teachers of God have found themselves like Joseph, behind bars for something they didn't do, because they would not be corrected in any other way.

Just imagine how cautious the Prophet Nathan had to be when the Lord sent him to King David to confront him over his sin with Bathsheba. Prophets throughout the Bible were directed to correct the world leaders of the day. Some like David repented, though there were consequences for his sin. Others disregarded the prophets completely. Some of the prophets were beaten, some were put in prison. Jeremiah was thrown into an empty well that was thick with mud at the bottom. Mud into which he sank. Some prophets were executed for giving the word of the Lord to a leader.

It may encourage everyone to know that ministering under the anointing of the Holy Spirit is something that gets easier as we learn to hear the Spirit's voice and yield to Him.

People unfamiliar with the ministry of the manifestation gifts can get frightened when someone operates under the anointing. This is especially true of visitors who may not be familiar with this kind of ministry in a service. When we operate under the anointing of the Holy Spirit, we don't have to make it overly dramatic. Simply standing and ministering as the Lord anoints us to do so is dramatic enough. When things like that happen, people tend to leave the church and never come back. They will also tell others what happened and discourage them from attending.

I know of a paramedic who was visiting a church where people were falling under the power of God. This man was unfamiliar with this kind of thing. He got up from his seat and began to administer first aid to the woman who was laying on the floor in the isle close to him. The ushers quickly came and escorted him out of the service. They could have used this as a teachable moment; instead, that man was asked to leave the church and he went away confused and embarrassed.

When operating these gifts, we are simply providing the vehicle through which the Holy Spirit is ministering. It is not about us; it is about Him! If others in the service can't understand what we are saying, or if we say it in such a way that it is disruptive, no benefit will be received from this ministry.

Believers should evaluate periodically as they learn to minister. If you are drawing attention to yourself in some way; if you are the only one ministering in a certain way; it is possible you need to change the method by which you minister. Your ministry will not be effective if you are operating in the flesh, or if you are disruptive. Not everyone is comfortable with the way the Holy Spirit ministers. I have relatives who visited our church once. I say once, because they were alarmed that the pastor went into the sanctuary and started anointing people and praying over them. Just doing that made them uncomfortable.

If the message you are presenting to the body is not backed by scripture, it is likely the person in charge of the service will ask you to stop speaking. Correction should always be done in love. If it is possible to correct someone after the service, that is when it should happen. In the case where leadership has already spoken with someone privately, and they refuse to be corrected, it may become necessary to lovingly deal with that person during the service. This is never to be the first step in correcting someone; it will be one of the last correctional steps taken.

I have been in churches where people were at the altar praying and a single individual began to pray loudly in tongues. This prayer was not interpreted. By doing this from the altar when others were receiving prayer for their needs, it would be out of order.

You know, life can be messy. There was a lady who was in a troubled marriage, and she was considering suicide. Her husband was addicted to drugs and he was a repeat adulterer. She had just tested positive for AIDS, and she was emotionally crushed. This lady started crying out to the Lord from the depths of her being in a service where she was seeking comfort and counsel from the Lord. The people around her were intolerant and they lacked compassion. Instead of ministering to her needs, she was asked to leave the service because she was being disruptive.

This lady left the church in great humiliation. As she was walking away from the church, the Lord sent a Spirit-filled woman her direction. This woman came up to her on the street and, sensing that this woman needed help, she invited her for coffee. The distressed woman opened up about her marriage, and how she was at her wits end. This Spirit-filled woman ministered hope and love; then she prayed with her. The women ended up turning her life over to the Lord, and started going to the Spirit-filled lady's church. It changed her life. This is an example of how the private operation of the manifestation gifts can operate to change lives. Be open to the Spirit when He places you in a position to minister to someone.

Let's be tolerant and loving when someone has a desperate need. Pray with someone like that. This is not the time to educate someone on how the services operate. Show anyone like this the love of Jesus and show that you care.

There are many angry people in the world today. They seem to just be waiting for someone to knock the chip off their shoulder. Men and women of God should be able to recognize through the gift of a word of knowledge what is going on in a troubled person's life, and do what they can to minister to those needs.

There is a learning curve for those who are new to ministry, and we should make allowances for mistakes. Please be open for someone in leadership to give pointers and instructions after you minister. How else are people to learn? Make the decision not to get your feelings hurt if corrected. What you view as correction might be simple suggestions to make your presentation better. We encourage everyone to learn about this ministry, but be open for some instruction and correction if needed.

It takes boldness to step out in faith to minister. It takes boldness and humility to receive correction. Understand that the person administering correction must have some boldness to be able to say and do what they must to correct someone. When correction is administered, it must be done in love, and every attempt should be made to avoid embarrassment.

Questions for Study and Discussion

1. Is it ever appropriate to minister through any of the manifestation gifts of the Holy Spirit in a church where those gifts are not recognized and practiced? Please explain.

2. Who is in charge of the service?

3. If you are speaking a word and the one in charge of the service tells you to be quiet, how should you respond?

4. When you are in a service and you sense the power of the Holy Spirit come upon you, does that always mean you are to speak out in a service?

5. Can the Holy Spirit gifts operate through someone who is not called to minister through them publicly? Explain.

CHAPTER 12

PROPHETS OUTSIDE OF THE PENTECOSTAL COMMUNITY

The manifestation gifts of the Holy Spirit are not denominationally restrictive, and neither are the five-fold ministry offices. Anyone who has been infused with the power of the Holy Spirit can operate through the manifestation gifts. Likewise, anyone who has been filled with the power of the Holy Spirit, and has been commissioned and anointed to do so, can operate or stand in one of the five-fold ministry offices no matter what denomination of Christian church they are associated with. Rather than speaking messages in a service, as they might do in a Pentecostal church, the Lord will most often use them through the private operation of the manifestation gifts. They may be able to speak direction and guidance from the Holy Spirit to the leadership of a church as a board member, elder, or both. The prophet may not speak what he is hearing from the Holy Spirit in the form of a message; but rather, he will tactfully and under the anointing of the Holy Spirit operate through the gift of a word of wisdom or the gift of a word of knowledge in a conversation with leadership. Likewise, the gift of discerning of spirits may operate to uncover wrong motives in the body of Christ.

There are people in the Evangelical and Catholic communities who have been called to the office of the prophet. These individuals may operate with very limited knowledge of the manifestation gifts because the gifts are not taught in these communities. That does not disqualify these individuals from being prophets, because the Holy Himself can and will teach them how they are to function in any of the offices to which they have been called, and within the church the Holy Spirit has placed them. They might operate more effectively if they understood the gifts of the Holy Spirit, but that does not restrict the Holy Spirit from operating through them.

Because most other churches do not recognize, and do not allow for the gifts of the Holy Spirit to operate in their services, the private operation of the manifestation gifts will allow them to serve the Lord in different ways as prophets. For years, I operated through the manifestation gifts of the Holy Spirit, and in the office of the prophet relying only on the voice of the Lord to guide and direct me in what I was doing and saying.

I believe many of the Evangelical and Catholic churches across this nation have active prophets operating in their congregations. There have been great evangelists that the Lord worked through powerfully who did not, speak in tongues that we know of, but the Lord used them in the office of the evangelist to bring many lost souls to the Lord. I believe the Lord has placed prophets in some political offices across this country giving them the opportunity to hear the voice of the Lord, and give the Lord's counsel to those in a place to act upon it. We worship the giver of the gifts not the gifts. We strive to be obedient to the Lord in whatever He directs us to do for Him.

Anyone who has accepted Christ as his Savior, and has received the Holy Spirit into their lives, can operate in the office of the prophet when God places His anointing upon them to do so. Understanding the manifestation gifts of the Holy Spirit enhances the prophet's ability to operate in this office. That is why they have been included in this teaching on the office of the prophet.

I believe there are individuals in many denominations who operate through the manifestation gifts of the Holy Spirit; they may not recognize they are operating through these gifts. That doesn't mean they are not hearing from the Lord. I have heard evangelical ministers speaking prophetic words through their sermons. The Pentecostal church in this nation does not have the market cornered on the office of the prophet. God is God and He will speak to His people and anoint them to speak for Him, whether or not they are in the Pentecostal community. Even the apostle Paul stated, "I would like every one of you to speak in tongues, but I would rather have you prophesy. The one who prophesies is greater than the one who speaks in tongues, unless someone interprets, so that the church may be edified" (I Corinthians 14:5)

God can speak to the unbeliever to bring them to salvation. Why then would He not speak to believers in all denominations? The more important question might be are these believers listening? There are many who seek to hear the voice of the Lord and when He speaks to them, they obey. I was raised in the Church of God. This was the Evangelical Church of God. They do not teach about, nor do they promote the Holy Spirit baptism; however, some of their members have been baptized in the Holy Spirit, and they do speak with other tongues in their prayer lives. This teaching is not emphasized in the Evangelical community, but that does not restrict the Holy Spirit from filling those who seek Him in these communities. I know of priests in the Catholic Church who have been filled with the Holy Spirit, and who hear from God. In fact, the charismatic conference my husband and I attended just after we got married was sponsored by the Catholic Church.

Throughout the years, many great gospel singers have come from the Evangelical community. The messages in many of their songs would lead one to believe that these individuals know what it is to be filled and infused with the power of the Holy Spirit. Many in my family still belong to the Church of God. I know my brother hears the Holy Spirit speaking to him. He talks to Him on a regular basis. He does not speak in tongues, but the Holy Spirit speaks to him. One must take the time to listen for the voice of the Lord to hear Him.

In these churches where the Holy Spirit and His manifestation gifts are not recognized, Spirit-filled believers may have the opportunity to minister through the private operation of the manifestation gifts as they pray, and counsel with troubled church members for God's touch in their life. The private operation of the manifestation gifts operates very effectively in cases like this. One does not need to announce they are operating through these gifts for them to operate effectively in many different ways.

Questions for Study and Discussion

1. Can believers outside of the Pentecostal community operate in the office of the prophet?

2. Why would prophets in religious communities other than the Pentecostal community operate differently?

3. Discuss how a prophet might minister effectively in a non-Pentecostal church.

CHAPTER 13

PROPHETS AND THE WORKING OF MIRACLES

Not all of the Lord's prophets worked miracles. At least there are prophets that do not have recorded miracles attributed to having occurred at their hand. The same goes for prophets today. Not all prophets in this day and age perform miracles. In fact, many do not perform miracles.

There were some big named prophets from scripture who did not have the gift of working of miracles operating in their lives. Prophets like, Daniel, Ezra, Nehemiah, Jeremiah, John the Baptist, and many others did not operate through the working of miracles as far as we know. The fact that not all prophets operate through the gift of working of miracles does not make them any the less prophets.

Daniel was able to interpret dreams, and give wise counsel through the power of the Holy Spirit, but he had no recorded miracles attributed to having been done by him. Of course, he received the miracle of being delivered from the lion's den. John the Baptist was commissioned to speak the revelation of the coming Christ before he was placed in his mother's womb, but he did not have any miracles attributed to him. Remember, prophets are messengers of God. Their lives are used by God as examples to the body of Christ. The things that a prophet endures over his lifetime speak as loudly as their words. The working of miracles is not a requirement for being a prophet of God.

I have seen the Lord miraculously provide for our family when there was no money to pay our bills, and He has provided food for our table. The Lord expects us to do all we can for ourselves when He is answering our prayers. The Lord provided mana in the wilderness for the people of Israel, but He still required the people to go out and harvest the mana. He did not cook it for them; they had to cook it for themselves.

Cash money has turned up in my mail box; this was money, the source of which I had no way of knowing, other than to believe it came from God. The Lord impressed family members to contribute large amounts of money when my husband lost his job in 1983. Money that was not supposed to be there has simply appeared in our checking account. We serve a powerful God who hears and answers prayer in miraculous ways. He is not restricted to the laws of nature or the laws of science.

The Lord answers prayers in several different ways. There are times when He hears our prayers, answers immediately, and just as we asked Him to answer. More often God requires us to wait for our answer. I don't know what governs how the Lord answers our prayers; I just know He doesn't always send our answers immediately. Perhaps the reason is as simple as there are lessons we need to learn before the Lord can answer our prayers, or there may be something we need to do before He can send the answer. There are times the Lord answers our prayers with a "no." This may be because what we are asking for would ultimately serve to harm us. He is God and we must trust Him to do whatever is best for us in all situations. Sometimes that means accepting no as the answer.

Questions for Study and Discussion

1. Do all prophets operate through the gift of the working of miracles?

2. Name some of the prophets from the Bible who did not have any miracles recorded having been done at their hand.

3. Discuss the different ways the Lord answers prayer.

CHAPTER 14

CHARACTERISTICS OF A PROPHET

Who me?

When God calls someone to be a prophet, He calls the most unlikely of people. In fact, the typical response of the one who is truly called to be a prophet is to say, "Who me? What have I got to offer as a prophet?" The true prophet will be humble in heart and recognize that there is no life in a message spoken by him, unless the Holy Spirit gives life to that word. The prophet will be willing to step aside, and let the Lord move through him. The true prophet, will be amazed at the power of the Holy Spirit, and the things He will accomplish through his obedience.

Conversely, the one who is eagerly asking God to appoint him to be a prophet will probably not be the one commissioned by God to minister in the office of a prophet. God chooses those who can be trusted to do what He tells them to do every time He speaks, and then to give the Lord, the glory for what was done.

When the Lord calls someone who is not humble to be His prophet, there will be a time of humbling. What do I mean by that? The Lord through life circumstances, will humble the proud so that he can be an effective messenger for the Lord. It will be a difficult time of learning that will cause a breaking of the human spirit, so that the Spirit of the Lord can rise up in that person. The Prophet Joseph comes to mind. He spent many years in prison being humbled before the Lord brought him into his true call and commission. Jonah is another one who was humbled by God. Jonah was a difficult case. For you in the body of Christ who are difficult cases, the Lord may have a large fish waiting for you!

God may use illness that is brought on by an individual's own lack of discipline in the way he lives his life. He may use the actions of family members; there is nothing more humbling than having the police call to tell a mother or father that they are holding their child for some horrible crime. God may not be the one who initiates these actions, but He will use them for His purposes. He can use financial ruin to humble an individual He has called to be His prophet. Again, He may not cause the financial ruin, but He will use it. When I say He may not cause these things to happen, you must understand that we often suffer from our own unwise choices; can you say self-sabotage? The precious Holy Spirit will use these same types of challenges in the lives of the lost or the backslidden to draw them to Himself as well.

The office of a prophet is not a call that elevates someone; instead, it is a high call to be the voice of God Almighty to the body of Christ elevating Him, not themselves. Often, those who seek the office of a prophet and ask God to appoint them to be prophets are seeking the recognition and approval of man for themselves. Others are looking only for the power that comes with the office of the prophet, but for their own purposes. These attitudes will lead to a ministry that will be easily corrupted.

In the Book of Exodus when God called Moses, his response to this high calling was essentially to say, "Who me?" He was talking to the Almighty God mouth-to-mouth, and instead of asking Him to heal his impediment, he asked God to provide someone to speak for him. Though God accommodated Moses, and appointed Aaron, his brother, to be the one to speak in his stead; it was Moses upon whom the strongest anointing of the office of the prophet was placed. No other prophet had a more powerful voice for the Lord.

In the Book of Jonah, you can find Jonah's response to being called by God was to run away. You should know that you can't run away from God, or hide from Him. He will find you and impress upon you the need to be obedient to His call. In Jonah's case He sent a very large fish to swallow him. While in the belly of the fish, Jonah had a change of heart. He repented and told God he would obey. God helped him out by having the fish deliver him to the shores of Nineveh. There was no opportunity to turn back.

A prophet sees right and wrong clearly.

When a prophet looks at a matter, there is no question in his mind. He automatically sees right and wrong with no wavering. God calls those to be prophets who can make a distinction between right and wrong (the holy and the profane). They seek after right, and will speak out against wrong. While those who are not prophets will ignore wrong or make some kind of excuse as to why it is okay to participate in sin, the prophet will be unequivocal, and declare that what is taking place is wrong. There is no compromise or justification for sin with one who has been called to be a prophet. Often a prophet will be too harsh in these situations. It takes maturity and the ability to seek the Lord for the appropriate love and mercy to properly state what is right and wrong.

Prophets will not stand for sexual sin, greed, wasteful living, promiscuity, adultery, pornography or any other immorality, neither will the One for whom they speak. If prophet participates in these activities, he will be disqualified to effectively minister in the office of the prophet, though he has been called and commissioned to do so. A prophet's life must be lived in righteousness as much as is humanly possible. If he indulges in sin, or participates in immorality, the Lord will not be able to effectively communicate through him. Though when the Lord can find no one else to speak for Him, He will use that corrupted prophet. Look at Samson for the proof of this.

"Flee from sexual immorality. All other sins a person commits are outside the body, but whoever sins sexually, sins against their own body." (I Corinthians 6:18) There is another scripture concerning this subject, "But among you there must not be even a hint of sexual immorality, or of any kind of impurity, or of greed, because these are improper for God's holy people. Nor should there be obscenity, foolish talk or coarse joking, which are out of place, but rather thanksgiving." (Ephesians 5:3)

We are all called to be examples of Christ in this world. For a prophet, this is more compulsory because he is the voice of God; his life is an example to the body of Christ. Anyone who ministers for the Lord should live his life in a pure and clean way. A prophet should not over indulge in drugs or alcohol. When drugs or alcohol are involved, the voice of the Lord becomes less clear. The lines between right and wrong become blurred. What you are hearing may not be from the Holy Spirit, but you will be unable to tell because your thinking is impaired. We are all humans, and we will all sin from time-to-time. It is vital when a prophet recognizes sin in his own life, he repents quickly so that he can be restored just as it was with the Lord's servant, priest, and prophet David.

In the body of Christ today, we have people who are called to be prophets of God, but they are not living according to the Word of God. It is quite acceptable in this day and age for a couple to live together without being married. They seem to have no qualms about having children without being married. However, this is against the Word of God, and one living in this situation must repent and turn from this wickedness before he can serve effectively in the office of the prophet, or any other office for that matter. Simply asking for forgiveness is not enough. Unless the decision is made to change and correct the way a life is being lived, one cannot speak for the Lord. Asking for forgiveness knowing that no life change is going to take place is not a true prayer of repentance. When we pray, God is listening to our heart as well as the words we are speaking. Repentance means turning away from the wrong. God cannot effectively use anyone who chooses to live in rebellion to Him. Understand, no one can live a pure, clean, and holy life without the help of the Holy Spirit.

I feel it necessary to approach a few additional types of sin that seem to be acceptable in the body of Christ today. This is not my own judgment; I believe the Lord wants me to be very specific here.

There are people in the body of Christ who legitimately had disabilities at one time or another in their lives. Because of those disabilities they began receiving financial benefits provided for such purposes. Either through healing or medical treatment, these people have been restored to health. Instead of notifying those responsible for distributing these financial benefits, they continue to collect financial help. This is a sin before God, and until true repentance is sought these individuals cannot be effectively used by God.

What these people should be doing is going out and finding gainful employment because they are now able to perform profitable duties. In the same way, we have people collecting food subsidies, but they are now gainfully employed. Instead of reporting that the food subsidies are no longer needed, they just continue to receive them. Some of these people actually sell their food subsidies to get money to purchase items other than food. This is against the law; and therefore, a sin before God.

Until these people are caught or the Lord makes them so uncomfortable that they can't stand it any longer, they cannot effectively minister in the office of the prophet. There are many other examples that we could talk about. There are people stealing time from their employer by reporting late for work, taking longer than allowed breaks, and leaving early instead of working a full eight hours. There are others who cheat their employer on their expense accounts. All of these types of sin will separate you from the powerful anointing of the Lord. These people proclaim to know God, but they have no testimony because those who are in the world see no difference between your life and their own. These are the type of Christian of whom it is said, "If that is a Christian, I don't want to have anything to do with Christianity."

Prophets love to worship.

Prophets of the Lord know how to step into the awareness of the Lord's presence. Music helps the prophet get in tune with the Holy Spirit. Multiple times in the Old Testament, the prophet called for music to be played so that he could step into the awareness of the Lord's presence, and hear from Him. Extreme worship is something that prophets thrive on. Worship music offered to the Lord as a sweet sacrifice can motivate the Holy Spirit to send His word to the congregation. Prophets who operate as worship leaders can minister very effectively to usher in the awareness of the Lord.

Participating in high praise and worship especially when a prophet is leading, can result in people being released from bondage. This type of release does not require any action other than to reach out to the Lord during these times. Healing and miracles can also be released during these times of high praise and worship.

In a private setting, music can cause the Holy Spirit to draw near to the prophet so that spiritual conversation can take place. King David sang to the Lord, and he wrote a great many of the Psalms. Reading those Psalms will enrich the prophet, and offering those psalms to the Lord as personal praise will cause the Lord to draw near. In an atmosphere where high praise and worship are taking place, the Holy Spirit will be motivated to make known His presence, not only through the prophetic word, but the prophet may receive revelation from the Lord during these times. Personally, nothing gets me into the awareness of the presence of the Lord faster than praise and worship that comes from deep within my heart.

Prophets see spiritual visions and dreams.

One of the ways God speaks to His prophets is through visions and dreams. but not all who see visions and dreams are called to be prophets. For those who serve in the office of the prophet, God communicates in very personal ways. Sometimes God speaks directly to His prophets, as He did with Moses when He commissioned him. Other times, God will send a spiritual dream or a vision; these communications are initiated by God not the prophet. The Lord knows best how to communicate with His prophet. Some visions and dreams are easily understood; other times prayer and fasting are required so that the full message can be received.

The Prophet has a heart of compassion and mercy.

God implants within His prophets an ability to show mercy and compassion in the most unlikely situations. When he sees sin taking place, his response is to pray to the Lord for mercy and compassion for those partaking in sin. Prophets do not justify sin when they see it, but they stand ready to minister the mercy of God to those involved in sin. God hates sin, but He loves the sinner. A prophet has a special ability from the Holy Spirit to separate sin from the one who is committing it, and speak restoration to that person. This is exactly what Nathan the prophet did when he was sent by God to confront King David about his adultery with Bathsheba in I Samuel 12.

Moses interceded for the people of Israel in Numbers 21:7, when the Lord sent snakes into the camp, and many were bitten and died because of sin. Moses frequently stood in the gap between God and the people of Israel, even going so far as to place his own life on the line. There is no greater demonstration of mercy and grace.

The gift of discerning of spirits is vital for prophets.

The gift of discerning of spirits dwells strongly in those called to be prophets. You might ask, "How do I know if the gift of discerning of spirits dwells strongly in me?"

Those who have the gift of discerning of spirits operating within them can see into the spirit realm when the gift is functioning. This gift is not always active in the life of a prophet; the Holy Spirit activates it from time-to-time. As I have said previously, this gift operates in the background of all that I do as a prophet. The prophet can see angels or demons when this gift is in operation. They can hear the voice of demons, angels, and God, Himself. They can also either in a dream, vision, or through actual happening receive transportation from one place to another. I haven't heard of this happening in this day and age, but it happened several times in the Old and New Testaments. When transportation occurs through a dream or a vision, it is by an operation of the manifestation gift of discerning of spirits. When a human being is actually lifted up by the Spirit of the Lord and taken to another location as an actual happening, it is by an operation of the manifestation gift of working of miracles. I say this because when this happens it goes against the laws of nature; therefore, it is a miracle.

Transportation happened often enough to Elijah that when Obadiah was told to go tell King Ahab that Elijah would appear to him that very day, Obadiah asked him why he was sending him to his death?

He was afraid that he would tell Ahab that Elijah would appear, but the Spirit of the Lord would take him someplace else. No one would be able to find Elijah, and Obadiah would be put to death. (I Kings 18) In these instances of transportation, Elijah was actually being carried from one place to another. It was through the manifestation gift of working of miracles since the transportation was an actual happening.

Ezekiel also experienced this supernatural event, "The hand of the Lord was upon me, and He brought me out by the Spirit of the Lord and set me in the middle of the valley; it was full of bones." (Ezekiel 37:1) This instance of transportation occurred through a vision making it an operation of the gift of discerning of spirits.

In the New Testament transportation by the Holy Spirit occurred when Philip was transported to another location. "When they came up out of the water, the Spirit of the Lord suddenly took Philip away, and the eunuch did not see him again, but went on his way rejoicing. Philip, however, appeared at Azotus and traveled about, preaching the gospel in all the towns until he reached Caesarea." (Acts 8:39-40)

In this instance Philip was carried from one location and deposited in another location where he went about preaching. This is a demonstration of the gift of working of miracles.

The Apostle John was transported in the Book of Revelation, "Then the angel carried me away in the Spirit into a wilderness." (Revelation 17:3) This demonstration of transportation by the Spirit occurred during a vision; therefore, it is a demonstration of the gift of discerning of spirits.

The gift of discerning of spirits is a key tool for those who minister in the office of the prophet, pastors, and those who minister in any way in the body of Christ. It is through this gift that the Holy Spirit will reveal those in the church who have wrong motivation.

There are times when a prophet meets someone, and has a supernatural understanding that the person has been deeply hurt in their life. He may meet someone, and recognize a spirit of some kind attached to them. He might sit down in a service, and begin to sense that someone nearby is in a sexually abusive relationship; he may not know who that person is, but the Holy Spirit who is in the prophet will make him aware that a sexually abusive spirit is there in the service. The prophet's obligation in situations like this is to bind the powers of darkness in the name of Jesus. When a prophet prays for someone to be healed, there can be an awareness that a spirit is attached to that person preventing the healing. The prophet in this case should bind satan, and break his power so that healing can be received. These are all examples of the gift of discerning of spirits in operation.

Waiting on the Lord is a priority for a prophet.

A prophet will have a deep longing to spend time in the awareness of the presence of the Lord. Many people in the body of Christ wait on the Lord; this does not necessarily mean that they are prophets. However, part of the call of the prophet is to spend copious amounts of time waiting on the Lord to hear His voice for the body of Christ or for a particular individual. The Lord may give a prophet a vision or a dream, and he will spend hours seeking the Lord for the full meaning of what he has seen. Prophets enter into the awareness of the Lord's presence, and they soak His presence in like a sponge absorbs water. They may not say anything; they simply bask in His presence.

Prophets seek after God. They desire to be in the Lord's presence. They wait upon Him to reveal His heart to them. They wait upon the Lord to reveal His thoughts. They wait on Him to speak to them about His desires for them, for the body of Christ, and for the nation.

"Even youths grow tired and weary, and young men stumble and fall; but those who hope in the Lord will renew their strength. They will soar on wings like eagles; they will run and not grow weary; they will walk and not be faint." (Isaiah 40:30)

"For My thoughts are not your thoughts, neither are your ways my ways, declares the Lord. As the heavens are higher than the earth, so are my ways higher than your ways, and my thoughts than your thoughts." (Isaiah 55:8-9)

Prophets are Intercessors.

Many people in the body of Christ are intercessors. God calls all believers to times of intercession. You might be a prophet if the Holy Spirit often places a burden upon you to pray. The Lord will encourage you to pray through a situation until the burden to pray lifts. There are times that the burden will last for weeks, months, or even years. Prophets, as intercessors, stand in the gap between God and the people. This means that the prophet pleads on behalf of the people before God.

"So, He said He would destroy them had not Moses, His chosen one, stood in the breach before Him to keep His wrath from destroying them." (Psalm 106: 23)

When the Lord places a burden upon you to pray, you should obey. Your prayer might change the course of history.

On a cold rainy night in December of 1985, my husband got called into work early. His shift was supposed to start at 11:00 p.m. He left the house around 9:00 p.m. I got the children into bed and sat down to relax for a few minutes before getting ready for bed. While relaxing, an intense burden to pray came upon me, but the Lord did not show me why I was praying. I began to pray in the Spirit using my prayer language. As I prayed, I began crying and urgently seeking the Lord for this situation that I knew nothing about. Around 10:15 p.m. the burden lifted and I went to bed.

Shortly after falling asleep, I was awakened by the phone. It was one of my husband's coworkers asking me if Charlie, my husband, was coming into work that night. I was startled and told his coworker that he had been called in early and left the house at 9:00 p.m. I told him that he should have been at work hours ago. He told me not to worry, that Charlie probably had a flat tire or something. I knew in my spirit that was not the case. I knew instantly it was my husband for whom the Lord had me praying.

At that hour of night, I didn't want to get the boys out of bed to go looking for my husband, so I called our neighbor, and told him that Charlie had not shown up at work. I asked if he would drive the route that he would have taken, and see if he could find his vehicle off to the side of the road. He agreed and I got on my knees and prayed again. This time the Lord did not have to place a burden upon me to pray; I knew the problem and I began to bombard the gates of heaven.

Several hours later I received the next phone call. My neighbor had found Charlie; he was with him at the hospital. They were sewing his kneecaps back in place. The neighbor told me that Charlie had been hit head on by a 15-year-old girl, traveling around 55 miles per hour, who had blown through a stop sign on the wet-rainy roads. Charlie had been traveling at around 35 miles per hour. He was in a little mini truck; the other driver was in a very large 4x4 Dodge, Ram. My husband had held on to the steering wheel so hard that it bent down to the steering column. His foot was broken when he stomped on the brake, and his kneecaps were torn out when the dashboard hit his knees. His shoulders were dislocated as were his wrists. The steering column impacted his chest, and had broken most of his ribs, and bruised his heart and lungs. The bruising caused his heart and lungs to swell making it impossible to take a breath. At the very time I had been called to pray so urgently, the paramedics were trying to bring him back to life. Twice on the way to the hospital they lost him. If I had not been obedient to the Lord when He called me to pray, my husband might well have died that night. He had a very long recovery ahead of him, but he was alive, and I knew it was an answer to my prayers.

Prophets are human and as such are flawed.

Just because someone is anointed to be a prophet of God it doesn't mean they are infallible, nor does it mean they are any more special than others. Prophets are human just as we all are. Throughout the scriptures, we see prophets who ran from God's call on their lives like Jonah. We see prophets who had problems with depression like Moses, Elijah and Jonah. There is an incident in II Kings 2:23-24, where Elisha called down a curse upon a group of boys when they teased him and jeered at him. This group of boys was from Bethel. When Elisha called this curse down on them, two bears came out of the woods and mauled forty-two of the boys.

When the Lord places His power upon His prophets, the prophets must be diligent to treat that power with reverence. Balaam loved money so much that he responded to Balak's call to curse the people of the Lord. Of course, the Lord became angry with him and gave a human voice to his donkey who then spoke to him to get his attention. Abraham passed Sarah, his wife off as his sister, to save his own skin. (Genesis 12:13) In Genesis 26:9, Abraham's son Isaac followed in his father's footsteps, and passed his wife off as his sister to save his own life as well.

King David is one of my favorite prophets; he was powerfully anointed of God. He was well known as a worshiper; he loved the Lord, but he fell to temptation, and committed adultery with Bathsheba. You can read this account in II Samuel 11. As if adultery were not enough, David conspired to kill Bathsheba's husband Uriah in battle so that he could take Bathsheba as his wife and cover his sin. He might just as well have pierced him with his own sword. By placing him at the front lines, other mighty warriors died as a result of his decision to kill Uriah in battle.

Again, David sinned before the Lord when he went against God's will and counted the people of Israel. He was responsible for the deaths of tens of thousands of people because of his disobedience to God. In spite of all the wrongs that David did, God called him a man after His own heart. Each time the Lord spoke to David about his sin, David was quick to repent and God forgave him. This should give everyone in the body of Christ encouragement when it comes to being restored after sinning in very deliberate ways.

Peter sinned when he denied Christ three times the night that Jesus was betrayed. As soon as the rooster crowed, Peter remembered that Jesus had told him he would deny Him, and he went out and repented with great remorse. Peter was forgiven as soon as he repented and God restored him. I remind you that in Acts 2, when the Holy Spirit was given, it was Peter who stood before the crowd of people that had gathered curious about what was happening. It was Peter who told the people that this was the Comforter that Jesus had promised to send, and he went on to tell the people about the good news of Jesus.

I believe Judas could have been forgiven if he had only repented and asked to be forgiven. There are many other examples of prophets being human. I encourage you to study the prophets. You will be surprised what you can learn.

One of the most important things to remember about being human as a prophet is to repent often, and spend time in the awareness of the Lord's presence so that the Holy Spirit can do His restoring work.

These demonstrations of frailties in the Lord's appointed prophets, give hope to those in the body of Christ who battle daily with guilt and shame over sins that they have committed. I believe our loving Heavenly Father gave us the examples of the humanity of the prophets to instill in the body of Christ that God really is forgiving and merciful toward His people. If the prophets can be forgiven so can all who will call upon the name of the Lord.

Prophets often hurt feelings.

It doesn't take a prophet to recognize that people do not like to be corrected. Often our first response to correction even from the Lord is to get hurt feelings. Prophets are not "yes men." They speak truth without sugar coating it; they call sin what it is, sin. If you are concerned about offending others, you will not make a good prophet. Prophets must have thick skin and not take it personally when others are offended at the words they speak or when others offend them. They must speak what God tells them to speak without apologies, allowing the Lord Himself to minister to them when offended. Remember it is the Lord's reputation, not that of the prophet.

There will be times when the Lord will correct people in a very loving way. He will extend mercy to them and gently restore them, but there are those who will not hear correction in this way. There will be times when the Lord sends a prophet to correct the leadership of a church and it will be a harsh word.

The prophet must give the word the Holy Spirit speaks exactly as the word is given. When correcting leadership, the Lord is not always as patient because leadership should know right from wrong. The prophet must be willing to give the harsh words as well as the pleasant ones. When correcting leadership, it should be done in private at least initially. It is not the prophet's assignment to cause division in the church. If the leadership does not receive the word and correct their behavior, the Lord may require a prophet to correct leadership in a very public way. If the leadership will still not hear the correction offered through the prophet, the Lord will use other means to correct them. There are men and women of God who have been arrested, tried, convicted, and sent to prison because they would not accept correction the Lord sent through His prophets.

I personally know of occasions where financial improprieties were taking place and other occasions where sexual sin was being committed against children in the church. This sin became known through the prophet; the authorities were called which resulted in those individuals being sent to prison.

The Lord has required me to speak correction to leadership several times throughout my time of ministry. I would rather be hit by a bus than speak correction to leadership or even to a member of the body of Christ, but it is the obligation of the prophet to speak the words the Lord speaks to them.

On one occasion, the Lord had me write a letter of correction to the pastor of the church I was attending. It was concerning his issues with honesty. Several times he had been caught in a lie; these were what he called "acceptable lies" because he was telling them so he wouldn't cause hurt feelings. When you are a pastor and you lie to your people, a trust issue develops that prevents them from believing anything you say.

After the pastor read the letter, he called me on the phone in the middle of a very busy workday at the engineering office where I was working. I could not respond very effectively because I was surrounded by coworkers who did not share or care about my faith. They were expecting me to do my job instead of taking time for a personal phone call. The pastor was very angry, and He wanted me to explain myself. My response to him was simply to say the Lord had directed me to send the message, and I suggested he reread the letter and pray over it.

He never said another word to me about the letter, but I found out later that for weeks after he received that letter, he would take it into the sanctuary and kneel at the altar weeping as he prayed. It was painful for me to write that word, and it was painful to be confronted over the word the Lord had given. However, the Lord did a powerful work in that pastor through my obedience.

Another time the Lord had me correct the children's church pastor over something he was doing that was absolutely against scripture. He wanted to raise funds for the Sunday school. He had the idea to divide the children into groups so they could compete to see which group could collect the most offering. This competition was to go on for a month; at the end the team that had given the most money would get a free visit to a local ice cream shop.

The way they were taking the offering was very public. Each team member would go forward and drop money into an offering plate and tell the pastor how much they had given so it could be credited to the appropriate team. The scripture is very clear about the way an offering is to be presented.

"So, when you give to the needy, do not announce it with trumpets, as the hypocrites do in the synagogues and on the streets, to be honored by others. Truly I tell you, they have received their reward in full. But when you give to the needy, do not let your left hand know what your right hand is doing, so that your giving may be in secret. Then your Father who sees what is done in secret, will reward you." (Matthew 6: 2-4)

He was teaching the children that if you give you get. He was also disregarding the teaching on the privacy of giving. Not only did this competition create hurt feelings, it was against God's word. I was required by the Lord to address this with the children's pastor. Thankfully, he heard what the Lord was saying, he canceled the competition, and corrected what he had taught the children. He could have become offended and rejected the word.

Some televangelists are guilty of soliciting money they don't truly need. Money sent to ministries like this has been used for personal gain. There have been televangelists over the years who were convinced that they needed things like a private jet for their ministry. Others needed money to expand the size of their property holdings. These people didn't give a second thought about taking the last dollar from a poor widow who couldn't afford her medications. One minister was using offerings that the Lord's people sent to his ministry to pay for extravagant gifts and trips for him and his lover. I can remember an air conditioned dog house and gold faucets purchased out of funds sent to the ministry. The plea for cash was so the work of the Lord could be funded. Listeners were told they would be blessed by giving their hard-earned dollars to their ministry. The love of money has been the downfall of many ministries. God sends His prophets with words to correct ministers like these. When the word the Lord sends through His prophet is not heard or heeded, often the Lord will send a harsher message. In all of these cases, these were people that started out with a healthy love for the Lord who fell to the love of money. Those who will not hear correction that the Lord sends will be dealt with.

The Lord does not always require a prophet to address sin in the church among the leadership. Often the prophet will pray over wrongs that are revealed and intercede before the Lord on behalf of the church.

Prophets pray, fast and call others to do the same.

Prophets pray and fast for the body of Christ and for the Lord's will to be accomplished on this earth. There are times when the Lord calls His prophets to declare a time of prayer and fasting for the body of Christ. There are many reasons why the Lord calls His people to fast and pray.

When there is sin in the body of Christ, God will sometimes have His prophets declare a time of fasting, prayer, and repentance. When the nation has sinned greatly and God is motivated to destroy it because of wickedness, the Lord may have His prophets declare a fast.

A church may be having financial problems, or there may be some kind of conflict within the church; the Lord will have His prophets call the body of Christ to fast and pray. When there is political discord or when authorities are requiring the people of the Lord to do things that are against the Word of God, the Lord will have His prophet call for fasting and prayer.

When elections are taking place and the direction of the government is potentially going to change, the Lord will have His prophet call for prayer and fasting. Prayer accompanied with fasting can move the Lord's hand when simply praying doesn't seem to be getting a response.

When the Lord's direction is needed by the leadership of the church concerning decisions that need to be made, the prophet and even church leadership may call the people of the Lord to a time of prayer and fasting. Following are examples of fasts being called to gain God's ear and favor:

Scripture records that the Prophet Ezra called for a fast to ask God for protection. It says, "I proclaimed a fast, so that we might humble ourselves before our God, and ask Him for a safe journey for us and our children, with all our possessions. I was ashamed to ask the king for soldiers and horsemen to protect us from enemies on the road, because we had told the king, 'The gracious hand of our God is on everyone who looks to him, but His great anger is against all who forsake him.' So, we fasted and petitioned our God about this, and He answered our prayer." (Ezra 8:21-23)

When the Jewish people were to be wiped out, Queen Esther had the Israelites pray and fast for three days so that she might find favor when she went before the King. Going into his presence could have brought about her death. Because the people fasted and prayed, the Lord did a powerful work and spared Esther from the King's wrath. Ultimately, Esther was able to intervene on behalf of the Jewish people and they were able to defend themselves against those who would have killed every last one of them.

"Consecrate a fast, call a sacred assembly, assemble the elders and all the inhabitants of the land to the house of the Lord your God, and cry out to the Lord." (Joel 1:14)

"Even now," declares the Lord, "return to me with all your heart, with fasting and weeping and mourning...Blow the trumpet in Zion, declare a holy fast, call a sacred assembly." (Joel 2:12, 15)

Prophets have sound judgment.

The more a prophet stands in God's counsel, the more the prophet will learn of God's ways and thoughts. The prophet will then be better able to make sound judgments based on God's will not the will of man.

"But if they had stood in my council, they would have proclaimed My words to my people and would have turned them from their evil ways and from their evil deeds." (Jeremiah 23:22)

A prophet who seeks the counsel of the Lord will be able to assist the body of Christ in making sound decisions. The prophet will take a matter to the Lord and He will counsel the prophet. For instance, if a body of believers is considering building a church or perhaps moving the church to another location, the prophet can go before the Lord to ask His counsel on the matter, and the Lord will speak to the prophet. There might be a split coming to the church that no one has the ability to know about. This split would have an impact on the financial stability of the church. Perhaps there is going to be an economic collapse. An economic collapse might impact the funds coming into the church. By having the prophet seek the Lord on this decision, the Lord can prevent financial ruin for the church by giving the Lord's word to wait.

When the Lord sends His counsel through His prophet, it is the obligation of the leadership to do as counseled by the Lord. It is not the duty of the prophet to take offense when the counsel the Lord has given is not accepted. It is the duty of the prophet to intercede on behalf of the leadership who rejected the Lord's counsel.

The Lord directs prophets to anoint for ministry.

Prophets hear the voice of the Lord, and they are required to act upon what they hear. The Lord uses His prophets to anoint and set people apart for various ministries.

In I Samuel 13:1 the Lord sent Samuel to anoint Saul to be king over Israel. When Saul sinned before the Lord, God sent Samuel to anoint David to be king in Saul's place. Now, it took many years for David to actually take the throne. In I Kings 1:39, Zadok the priest anointed Solomon king in David's place.

People talk about placing their prophet's mantel upon someone. The only time I can find the mantel referred to in scripture with regard to the prophet is in I Kings 19:19. Elijah was told by God to go and anoint Elisha to be a prophet. "Elijah went up to him, and threw his cloak (or mantel) around him." This indicated that Elisha was being called or commissioned to be a prophet.

The full power of the Holy Spirit was not on the mantel. There might have been some residual anointing, but the mantel was simply used as a symbol that the anointing to serve in the office of the prophet was being placed upon Elisha. Elijah took his cloak back after he did this. Elijah spent the next period of time mentoring Elisha. Just before the Lord took him into heaven, Elijah asked Elisha what he could do for him. Elisha requested a double portion of the anointing that was upon Elijah. He was not asking this because he wanted power for himself. What he was asking was that he might do more for God's kingdom than Elijah had done. He was asking to be Elijah's successor as a strong and powerful prophet of God. This was a request that God himself would have to grant, if it were to be granted at all. Elijah essentially told Elisha that he would know that God had granted his request if he was present with Elijah when God took him.

Elisha was, in fact, present with Elijah when he was taken into heaven, and when his cloak fell to the ground, Elisha picked it up. This symbolized as it were the changing of the guard or the passing of the torch; Elisha was granted a double portion of the anointing that was upon Elijah as he had requested of the Lord. The mantel did not carry or transfer the anointing, it was simply symbolic that the Lord had granted Elisha's request to serve as the successor to Elijah and to do even more powerful work for God Almighty than Elijah had done.

Elijah raised people from the dead, he called down fire from heaven that devoured people, he healed people, he parted water and was transported by the Holy Spirit from place to place many times. These were just some of the wonders that were done by God as He operated through Elijah. Elijah had a powerful anointing from the Holy Spirit, and the anointing that was upon Elisha was double the anointing that had been upon Elijah. Elisha performed many wonders under the power of the Holy Spirit. The first wonder he performed after Elijah was taken into heaven was to part the waters of the Jordan River. He purified poisoned waters, raised a dead boy to life, he multiplied food as Jesus did in the New Testament, he healed Naaman the leper, he blinded an entire army, and did many more wonders. In fact, the anointing was so strong that even when Elisha died, there was so much residual anointing upon his body that when a dead man was thrown into his grave, that man came back to life. (II Kings 13:21)

I have been called by the Holy Spirit to place a commission and anointing upon several people throughout the years as I have ministered in the office of the prophet, and it is an awesome responsibility. This is not something that should be entered into lightly. It is something that is done after much prayer and direction from the Lord. Understand, when the Lord calls a prophet to anoint someone and commission them for ministry, the prophet cannot make them accept that anointing and act upon it. The prophet does not choose who to anoint. The Lord places a burden on a prophet or directs a prophet to anoint someone.

When the Lord has directed me to anoint someone, I have brought other names to Him. These were individuals who in my own eyes looked as though they might qualify as well. The Lord has been very specific with His direction to only anoint the one whose name He had given. The prophet is only responsible to do what the Lord has called him to do. It is up to the individual to embrace the anointing. Also, the Lord will send multiple confirms to the one who has been anointed.

The prophet can mentor someone and assist that person to experience the fullness of the office the Lord has called them to serve in, but the prophet cannot mature them. This is something that the Lord through His Holy Spirit will bring fully to the person that has been anointed when they come before Him and seek His face.

There is something else that everyone needs to understand. Education is a wonderful thing; I encourage those who minister for the Lord to get biblical education whenever possible, but for a prophet the Holy Spirit is the most important teacher. No amount of education can replace the powerful teaching that comes from the Holy Spirit Himself.

The Holy Spirit will develop the prophetic voice within the prophet. It is not necessary to copy the method used by someone else to present the word of the Lord to the body of Christ. The Holy Spirit will guide and direct how a word is to be presented. The Lord does not require His prophets to use theatrics to get the attention of the Lord's people. The power and authority that the Lord places within the prophet is all that is needed.

Questions for Study and Discussion

1. What is the typical response when the Lord calls someone to be a prophet?

2. What type of person does the God call to be a prophet?

3. When the Lord calls someone who is not humble to be a prophet, what must happen before that person can step into the office of the prophet?

4. How does the Lord humble believers who are proud?

5. Why would someone who has not been anointed and commissioned to be a prophet, seek to operate in the office of the prophet?

6. How did Jonah respond to God's call to go and preach to the people of Nineveh?

7. How did God change Jonah's mind?

8. How does a true prophet respond to right and wrong?

9. How should those who minister for the Lord live?

10. Why should a prophet be concerned about over indulging in drugs or alcohol?

11. Why is music important to the prophet?

12. Does a believer need to be a prophet, to see spiritual visions and dreams.

13. How should a prophet respond when he sees sin taking place?

14. Which of the manifestation gifts are in operation when a prophet receives transportation from one place to the other?

15. There was one prophet in the New Testament who was physically transported by the Holy Spirit from one place to another. Who was he?

16. A donkey spoke to which prophet?

17. Which prophet did God call a man after His own heart?

18. What is one of the most important things a prophet needs to remember about being human?

19. Discuss reasons why a prophet might call people to fast and pray.

20. Who is the most effective teacher for the prophet?

CHAPTER 15

SUFFERING

Suffering is something that prophets rarely talk about but it is something that I feel the church at large needs to understand. The life of a prophet is used by God as an example to the body of Christ. Often these examples are to call attention to the evil and wickedness taking place in the world around them. God uses the lives of His prophets to demonstrate to the people of God how their actions are viewed by him. He also uses life circumstances to keep His prophets humble. For this reason, the lives of the Lord's prophets were and are often filled with varying degrees of suffering.

Examine the life of Moses. When Moses obeyed the Lord as directed by Him to lead the people of Israel, the people complained and called his actions into question. The Lord had to speak to him often just to inspire and motivate him. We will speak later about the prayer Moses prayed to the Lord concerning the heavy burden God placed upon him. Moses received no praise or thanks from the people of Israel for his obedience to God. Likewise, the people gave no thanks to the Lord for His guidance and provision, just complaints. They needed food and when the Lord provided it, they complained because they didn't like what the Lord was serving. Then it was water, they needed water and complained again to Moses. The peoples' behavior was so frustrating to Moses that when the Lord caused water to flow from the rock it cost Moses his place in the Promised Land. He was so angry that he struck the rock instead of tapping it as the Lord had instructed. Since the rock was a symbol of Jesus, it was as if he struck the Lord and had to be disciplined by God for his actions.

The prophet Elijah spent many years isolated from the people of Israel because the king sought to kill him. And yet, the Lord used him in a powerful way to show the prophets of Baal that God was the one true God. Then Elijah had all the prophets of Baal slain. Jezebel, Ahab's wife, was so angry that she ordered that Elijah be hunted down and killed. This is the same prophet who called fire down from heaven to consume two troupes of soldiers, who now fled in terror.

Let's look at the life of Jacob's son Joseph. Joseph was raised in a home where his brothers hated him. His father loved him, but all of his brothers hated him enough that they plotted to kill him. It must have been a very difficult life, everything he did was called into question. His brothers were jealous and acted cruelly toward Him. Joseph was sold into slavery by his brothers; add to that, he spent years in prison because he was falsely accused of sexual assault. However, God had a plan.

The prophet Hosea was told by God to marry a prostitute (Hosea 1:2). God used Hosea's life as an example to the people of Israel who bowed to other gods and had sold themselves for the pleasures of the world. The Lord not only uses the words His prophets speak; He uses their lives as examples. When Hosea married Gomer, she did not give up her life of prostitution. It must have been a true torment to Hosea. Can you imagine trying to operate as a prophet of God while dealing with a wife who lived as a prostitute? Can't you imagine the ridicule that must have been showered upon him? He suffered further humiliation by having to pay Gomer to have relations with him in Hosea 3:2.

Under this topic of suffering, we must include the suffering of the royal family when they were captured by King Nebuchadnezzar as recorded in the Book of Daniel. Suffering comes in many ways. What a vivid example it was to all the heathen nations when Shadrach, Meshach and Abednego were thrown into a blazing furnace of fire and God delivered them. God also used Daniel's life to demonstrate the awesome power of God when He delivered him from the lions' den. The Lord God used these demonstrations of suffering in the lives of His anointed servants to prove the true power of the one true God.

Today there are prophets who go through personal suffering that remains unknown to the body of Christ. Powerful people of God, who strive to please the Lord and be obedient to Him, can have horrible trials in their personal lives. I am going to give some examples of situations that could take place in the life of a prophet.

The spouse of an anointed prophet may not know the Lord and fails to recognize or acknowledge the anointing of the Lord upon the spouse. A husband or wife may work to sabotage and undermine their spouse who is an anointed prophet. By doing this they are actually sabotaging the work of the Lord in the world today.

As an example of what God may require of a prophet today, I am going to tell you a story. There was a female prophet who was anointed and commissioned by God. Her husband turned away from the Lord after they married. He betrayed his wife by violating their marriage vows and committing adultery multiple times throughout their marriage. For a prophet it is not as simple as getting a divorce. God uses the lives of His prophets to demonstrate the sin and evil that is taking place in the world at large. Just as Hosea stayed in his marriage, this prophet stayed in the marriage at the Lord's direction. For these prophets, obedience to God is more important than a comfortable living environment. Don't you think it would be very difficult to live a godly life and hear the voice of the Lord while in a situation where a spouse is living a life of infidelity? Yes, divorce is always an option, but when the Lord tells a prophet to stay in the marriage, that is what the prophet should do. Trust in a situation like this is in the Lord alone. Forgiveness is required; it is the Holy Spirit who ministers to the prophet giving the ability to forgive. Any ordinary woman would probably have divorced her husband in this situation and who would blame her! A prophet must be obedient to the Lord.

There could be prophets who are married to drug addicts or alcoholics. The life of a prophet is lived in humility before God and in obedience, no matter what is going on in the home. I will say that the Lord does not always require prophets to stay in a marriage like this.

Scripture says, "And if a woman has a husband who is not a believer and he is willing to live with her, she must not divorce him. For the unbelieving husband has been sanctified through his wife, and the unbelieving wife has been sanctified through her believing husband. Otherwise, your children would be unclean, but as it is, they are holy." (I Corinthians 7:13-14) Sanctified in this scripture means made holy. By divorcing the unbelieving spouse, one could make the argument that the Lord's sanctification would be lifted from the unbelieving spouse since divorce severs the relationship. To the prophet obedience to the Lord is the most significant factor.

In another example, where infidelity is involved, the prophet has a heart-to-heart talk with the Lord. He is very honest with the Lord in his prayer. He tells the Lord that he does not want to lose the Lord's anointing no matter what is required. He asks the Lord for His wisdom concerning the situation. In this instance the Lord's response is that the anointing would not be lifted if divorce was the choice, but the prophet is challenged by the promise of a greater blessing in forgiving and working to restore the marriage. The prophet must seek the Lord's counsel in situations like this and then follow the Lord's direction.

Here is another example of how the Lord operates in the marriage of the prophet. The economy takes a downturn and the prophet is laid off. His wife continues to work trying to make enough money to pay the bills. The prophet seeks the Lord's direction but none seems to come. The prophet finds himself in a position where his house is foreclosed, and the family becomes homeless. It is a humbling experience for the entire family. You might ask why the Lord would allow this adversity to occur. Prophets are not above the trials of life. Prophets trust in the Lord to provide their needs no matter what the situation. The Apostle Paul says it best, "I am not saying this because I am in need, for I have learned to be content whatever the circumstances. I know what it is to be in need, and I know what it is to have plenty. I have learned the secret of being content in any and every situation, whether well fed or hungry, whether living in plenty or in want. I can do all things through Him who gives me strength." (Philippians 4:11-13)

Periodically there are news stories about pastors, teachers, and even prophets being accused of sexually inappropriate behavior towards a young person they were trying to help. Some of these accounts are undoubtedly true, only God knows the truth in situations like this. However, some of these individuals have found themselves behind prison bars though they did nothing wrong. You might say that is ridiculous! God would not allow that kind of punishment for an anointed man or woman of God. I remind you of Joseph who spent years in prison on an accusation of attempted rape. If God needs a man or woman of God inside a prison, He will allow them to be incarcerated to accomplish His purposes. If you think there are no believers behind bars think again. Prophets who go through hardships like this will often get angry at the Lord and lash out at Him. Then they will usually repent for their anger after a time and wait for the Lord to reveal the purpose for this adversity and for Him to deliver them.

Prophets may be required to minister to the needs of a handicapped child or children in their own homes while they operate as prophets for the Lord. Others minister to the needs of disabled family members. These individuals may be required to bathe and dress an adult family member and assist them in other ways. They minister to their loved one's physical and emotional needs as well. They will also be obedient to the Lord when He calls them to His service.

In my own life, our family has encountered financial situations requiring us to leave everything behind and start over in a new state, a state that neither of us had ever even visited. My husband lost his job working in a steel mill in 1983. He had worked there for more than 10 years when the decision was made to move production to Baytown, Texas. My husband's mother was bedridden at the time, and he did not want to leave the area. He remained unemployed for more than two years. When he finally got a job, it was in the state of Georgia. He was required to move ahead of the family to start his job; I was left behind to continue working for a time, take care of our two boys, and sell everything we had including our house. I will never forget packing all our worldly belongings into a rented 5 x 8 tow-along trailer. Pulling away from the house the boys began crying, as they saw many of their toys outside the house left by the garbage can because there was no room for them in the trailer. It was heartbreaking! Suffering comes in many ways.

In January of 2000 I was involved in an automobile accident sustaining a brain injury. I was unable to focus my eyes for more than three months and as result I lost my job. This injury affected my brain in several ways. After my eyes cleared up, I had short-term memory issues. I would be driving to an appointment and forget where I was going. I would have to pull over until my mind cleared and I remembered where I was going. Sometimes I would show up at the wrong doctor's office. I found myself paying bills twice and other bills didn't get paid at all. I had word retrieval issues, and had to learn to write all over again. These are just a few of the physical problems I have been through. In all of these situations, the Lord has continued to speak to and through me.

During the time I was recovering from this brain injury my husband was diagnosed with several physical issues. My being unable to work at the time made it possible for me to take him to various medical appointments for treatment. He spent weeks in the hospital having several surgeries during this time. When they sent him home from the hospital, he had to have a home nurse to administer medications. On one occasion I was in town shopping when a propane truck overturned on our road, and the fire department closed the road for hours. They sent the home nurse away leaving me to administer his IV medication.

After recovering from the brain injury, I was hired to work in a prison. I started out as a clerk in the sex offender treatment program inside the prison. These men were not locked down in cells as you might expect; instead, this portion of the prison had housing units designed as dorms. I had an office in the facility, but I could not close the door to the office due to security concerns. I was doing my work as a purchasing clerk while the sex offenders were having their group therapy sessions right outside my door.

If you don't think the Lord has a sense of humor, think again! During my time at the prison, I worked in several areas including the mental health area located in the super max unit. You might question why I have included this information under suffering. I viewed this portion of my life as suffering; working inside a prison is a toxic environment and it was dangerous. The stark reality of having freedom taken away became very real to me.

On my way home from work after the first day, I asked the Lord if I had heard Him correctly when He sent me to work inside a prison. He reminded me of how out of control I had been as a child, and how He had miraculously delivered me from being sent to a juvenile facility as a young person. He told me that if I had been sent to that juvenile facility, my life would have turned out differently. He said that if He had not intervened in my life at that point, the juvenile facility would have prepared me to be housed in a facility like the one in which He had sent me to work.

When my husband became disabled in September of 2006, I had worked at the prison long enough to accrue sick and annual leave allowing me the opportunity to accompany him to his various medical appointments. Some of those appointments were as far away as Lubbock, Texas.

As a prophet, I have been threatened with arrest for doing things the Lord directed. I once had a shotgun pointed at me while I was doing what the Lord directed me to do. I have been asked not to minister when the Lord was directing me to minister. I have been accused of practicing witchcraft for speaking the words the Lord told me to speak. My motives have been called into question for being obedient to the Lord. I have been defamed, rejected, laughed at, and accused of being a false prophet. All while doing what the Lord Almighty directed.

Though there have been many trials and tests in my life, I would not change a thing. I am where the Lord has me, and I am doing what He has placed before me to do. I praise Him for each trial and challenge He has used to mature me and teach me about His grace, mercy, and provision in my life.

Questions for Study and Discussion

1. Why do prophets suffer?

2. When Moses obeyed the Lord and led the people of Israel out of Egypt, what did the people of Israel do?

3. How did God provide water for the people of Israel in the wilderness?

4. Why was Moses not permitted by God to go into the Promised Land?

5. Why did Elijah spend many years in isolation?

6. The brothers of which prophet sold him into slavery?

7. Which prophet was told to marry a prostitute and why?

8. Did the prostitute stop selling herself to other men when she married Hosea?

CHAPTER 16

DISTINGUISHING BETWEEN TRUE
AND FALSE PROPHETS

There are many scriptures that deal with false prophecy. Just one of them is found in Jeremiah 23. I encourage everyone to read this chapter for themselves. I am going to include just verses 25-30.

"I have heard what the prophets say who prophesy lies in My name. They say, 'I had a dream! I had a dream!' How long will this continue in the hearts of these lying prophets, who prophesy the delusions of their own minds? They think the dreams they tell one another will make My people forget My name, just as their ancestors forgot My name through Baal worship. Let the prophet who has a dream recount the dream, but let the one who has My word speak it faithfully. For what has straw to do with grain?' declares the Lord. 'Is not My word like fire,' declares the Lord, 'and like a hammer that breaks a rock in pieces?'"

This scripture indicates that people have been giving false prophecy since Moses walked on the earth. In the Old Testament, a false prophet would be executed. This entire chapter in Jeremiah talks extensively about this problem. I documented previously the physical responses I experience in my body when the anointing of the Lord comes upon me.

When a prophet or a believer receives true prophecy from the Lord, it is like a fire burning within them. It can't be ignored. It will burn within them until the words are spoken, and when they are spoken, it will hit people who receive those words like a hammer.

In the New Testament, Jesus warned of false prophets. Understanding what a true prophet is helps the body of Christ to recognize the false ones.

God commanded the Israelites, "You shall have no other gods before me. You shall not make for yourself an image in the form of anything in heaven above or on the earth beneath or in the waters below. You shall not bow down to them or worship them; for I, the Lord your God, am a jealous God." (Exodus 20:3-5)

There are people in the body of Christ today who are worshipping false Gods. Some of these individuals were brought up in religious communities where they were encouraged to pray to things other than the Lord God. For instance, there are people who pray to family members who have passed away; others pray to dead religious figures that had great power from God while they were on the earth. There is only one God; He is alive and He hears and answers prayer.

Nothing made by man can be a true God and if you find yourself praying to anything or anyone but God it is idol worship. The commandment clearly states, "You shall have no other Gods before me." (Exodus 20:3) Those things do not have the ability to hear or answer prayer. There are others who elevate things in their lives that become as gods; examples of this could be their job, family, their status in the community, and certain personal possessions like houses or cars. Anything in your life that becomes more important than God Himself is an idol, and it is a sin before God.

As a prophet I am responsible to address sin where I see it. Make no mistake these sins are occurring in the body of Christ today. Please take this warning; if you are praying to anything other than the Lord God Almighty you are practicing idol worship. If you allow created things to be more significant in your life than the Lord God who created all things, you are guilty of idol worship.

A false prophet will often try to point the Lord's people to other gods or to himself acting in the role of a god. He might acknowledge that

Jesus was a prophet but deny the divinity of Jesus and the power of the blood of Christ. If someone says they are a prophet, but does not recognize Jesus Christ as the Son of God or fails to recognize that the blood of Jesus made redemption available to all mankind, he is a false prophet.

Some imposters will recognize the Bible, but add an additional religious book that must also be followed. A false prophet in the church can cause confusion by twisting scripture to alter its meaning or simply make things up and refer to those things as scriptural. False prophets have caused splits in the body of Christ by introducing false teachings. A lack of biblical knowledge has enticed people to believe in charlatans like Jim Jones, who went so far as to declare himself as Christ.

I once attended a church where the pastor was teaching about being baptized into what he called the "ascension level" of Christ. He was doing this by requiring members of his congregation to get up early in the morning, and go to a local river where he would immerse them in the water stating, "I baptize you into the ascension level of Christ." I do not find this baptism anywhere in scripture!

The scripture talks about water baptism that indicates an individual is dying to the things of the world, and as an outward profession of their faith. Scripture talks about the baptism in the Holy Spirit, where the believer is infused with the power of the Holy Spirit. I don't find any mention of a baptism into an ascension level of Christ. We don't need to make things up to encourage people to step into a deeper level with Christ. The Bible does not teach this ascension level of Christ; the pastor went further to rebuke those in the congregation who were unwilling to submit to this third baptism. This teaching split that church.

This church had previously taught salvation, water baptism, and the baptism of the Holy Spirit. When the pastor got into this false teaching, his actions proved him to be a false prophet. I remember that this same man who declared himself to be a prophet, grew a beard and showed up for church wearing a robe and carrying a staff showing himself as a type of Christ. A true prophet will have a check in their spirit when they encounter false prophets such as I have described.

Understand that satan has a counterfeit for all the manifestation gifts of the Holy Spirit, and it is satan who sends false prophets to confuse the body of Christ. He uses many of the same tricks that have worked since the earth was created. Scripture says, "For everything in the world, the lust of the flesh, the lust of the eyes, and the pride of life come not from the Father, but from the world and its desires pass away; but whoever does the will of God lives forever." (I John 2:16) Another scripture states, "Don't be deceived, my dear brothers and sisters. Every good and perfect gift is from above, coming down from the Father of the heavenly lights, who does not change like shifting shadows." (James 1:16-17)

The entire body of Christ needs to pray and guard against satan. Believers and most of all prophets, need to learn to distinguish the voice of the Lord in order that He will be obeyed. This is why the gift of discerning of spirits is so indispensable to the prophet.

Differentiating between a true prophet, and a false one becomes much easier through the gift of discerning of spirits. When this gift is in operation, a believer will be able to recognize when a true prophet is speaking the word of the Lord. This gift will allow a believer to detect if a prophet is speaking out of faith or if he is speaking true revelation from God. A true prophet will be known by his fruit and he will always point to the Almighty God.

I know of evangelists who started out their ministry being used by the Holy Spirit in powerful ways. As their ministries grew, they began to "help the Holy Spirit" by embellishing. They were faking the operation of the manifestation gifts by finding out about the needs of people who were attending their meetings through trickery. These false evangelists would do things like planting microphones in public areas of their facility in an effort to gather information. This information was used to fake words of knowledge by targeting the very needs that people had talked about. Still others used deep fitting ear buds with an accomplice backstage to relay the needs that had been overhead. It was all very dramatic, but these false evangelists were deceiving the people for their own glory and financial benefit. When these tactics were discovered, the ministry was discredited.

Evangelists have done things like waving their hands or blowing over a group of people in the audience in an effort to demonstrate God's power by having these people fall under the power of the Lord. This can and does happen. When the gift of discerning of spirits is in operation, believers can through this gift ,know if what the evangelist is doing is real or fake. This also goes for any theatrics that people make up to try to "help the Holy Spirit." My husband was once attacked by a band of what he called, "Wild Pentecostals" intent on forcing him to the ground. He wanted no part of this charade and fought back, embarrassing a few.

When Moses was called by the Lord, He was given powers to perform miracles. The magicians of the day were able to duplicate almost all of the miracles Moses performed. When Jesus came, He performed miracles, signs, and wonders. However, if you use miracles, signs, and wonders as a method by which to determine if someone is a prophet, you will be easily deceived. If a person is performing miracles, signs, and wonders but is pointing to another God, to the universe, to nature, or anything other than the Lord God Almighty, that person is a false prophet. The gift of discerning of spirits is used to differentiate between a true prophet of God and the false prophet.

There are mediums and fortune tellers that draw their power from satan. You will never hear these people say the Holy Spirit is speaking to them and revealing something. They say something like, "spirit is saying." Using the term "Holy Spirit" might just cause them to melt like wax.

It is repugnant to me to see television shows that depict mediums or fortune tellers operating in ways I know from experience the Holy Spirit operates. These are false prophets faking to have power that comes from God when what they are actually doing is drawing their power from satan through familiar spirits. Make no mistake about it they do have power, but it is not power derived from the Holy Spirit. The Holy Spirit operates to set people free from bondage, encourage, and heal. It is through the gift of discerning of spirits that believers can know the source of the power being demonstrated. There are only two sources of supernatural power in the universe, God Almighty and satan.

Not all prophets in this world are prophets of God. Some of them are prophets established by satan. In scripture, the god Baal had prophets. I'm sure there were many other gods that also had prophets. It is through the gift of discerning of spirits that these false prophets are detected.

Questions for Study and Discussion

1. What are some of the ways you can distinguish a false prophet from a true prophet of God?

2. Can satan operate through the manifestation gifts of the Holy Spirit? Explain.

3. Why do believers and prophets of God need to learn to recognize the voice of the Lord?

4. Do believers need to be able to recognize the voice of satan? Explain.

5. Which of the manifestation gifts of the Holy Spirit helps the believer determine if someone is a false prophet?

6. A true prophet of God will be known by what?

7. Who will a true prophet of God point to?

8. If a person is performing miracles, signs, and wonders, but is not pointing to the Lord God Almighty, he is what?

CHAPTER 17

THE CALL TO THE OFFICE OF PROPHET

There are believers in the body of Christ who operate through the manifestation gift of prophecy, but they do not know the difference between the office of the prophet and the gift of prophecy therefore confusing what their ministry truly is.

Everyone needs to understand that operating through the manifestation gifts is a function of the Holy Spirit. Failing to recognize this, diminishes these very significant methods God uses to meet needs in the body of Christ. The Holy Spirit recognizes those who have the faith and willingness to operate through the manifestation gifts, and He will frequently use these individuals in the body of Christ.

Each of the manifestation gifts has benefit, and I encourage all who have been filled with the Holy Spirit to learn about these gifts and how they function in the body of Christ. It is a blessing when the Holy Spirit operates in this way through a Spirit-filled believer. It benefits the body of Christ when a believer yields to the Holy Spirit.

A believer operating through the manifestation gifts is not necessarily a prophet. Simply prophesying does not make someone a prophet as we have previously discussed, but prophesying is a gift that benefits the body of Christ. Those who minister through one or more of the five-fold ministry offices (apostles, prophets, teachers, evangelists, and pastors) do so after the Holy Spirit calls and anoints them to minister in that way.

There are people in the body of Christ who are willing to step into a ministry simply because there is a need. For instance, there may be a need for a teacher, and a believer volunteers to fill the need. He can do this even though he has not been called to stand and minister in the office of a teacher. God will honor his willingness to serve God in this manner. No doubt there are pastors who have never truly been called and anointed by the Holy Spirit to minister in the office of a pastor. They may be doing this because there was a need, and no one was stepping forward to fill that need. God will still honor someone's willingness to pastor a congregation even without a call from the Holy Spirit.

So, you may ask, how do people know if they are a prophet or if they are simply called to minister through the manifestation gifts? The answer is simple but it is important. Only those who have been called and commissioned by God are true prophets. As you read and study the scriptures, you will learn the various ways God Himself placed His anointing upon various people as He commissioned them to serve as prophets of God.

The Lord calls His prophets based on His timing. It may be many years before that call is actually established in the life of God's chosen one. Each instance where the Lord called and commissioned someone to be a prophet was different. Most of those called to be prophets responded to the Lord in the same way. They said, "Who me?" Then they rattled off their list of reasons why they were unqualified for such a call.

Abraham fell down and laughed when God told him for the second time that He would be the father of many nations. Jonah did a complete 180, running the other direction. Moses said he didn't speak well enough to be a prophet of God, Jeremiah told God he was too young, and Isaiah told God he was a man of unclean lips. Samuel was called by God to be a prophet when he was just a young boy, but he did not walk in the fullness of that call for years.

David was called to be a prophet and king of Israel when he was only a teen. The Lord did not bring him into the fullness of that call until many years later, but David worked miracles through the power of the Holy Spirit even before he stepped into the prophetic call.

In Genesis 37, you can find the account of Joseph's dreams. Joseph was called to be a prophet through the dreams he had. Joseph bragged to his family about his dreams, The Lord commissioned him to provide for His chosen people when he was just a young man. Before he could fully step into that call, he had to suffer in many ways. The Lord actually used the hardship in Joseph's life to humble and mature him. It is good to remember that not everything the Lord speaks or shows to His prophets is to be shared.

When Joseph was sold into slavery, it humbled him. He could have chosen to be bitter and hate his brothers; instead, he chose to be the best slave he could be. When he was falsely accused of attempted rape and sent to prison for many years, Joseph could have spent his time being depressed or being bitter toward God for allowing all the hardships in his life. He did not do that; instead, he was the best prisoner he could be. He continued to worship God, and he continued to hear from God. We know this by the fact that he was able to interpret dreams even while he was in prison.

The same God who called Joseph to be His prophet allowed him to be imprisoned for a crime he did not commit. Now, consider that if Joseph had not spoken about his dreams, his brothers might not have sold him into slavery, and there would have been no one in place to interpret Pharaoh's dream that revealed the coming seven years of famine. I want to remind everyone our God works in mysterious ways to accomplish His purposes. God did not cause these events to take place, but He used these difficult events to provide for His people.

Usually, God appoints and anoints those who are humble in heart and willing to be obedient to the voice of God, while giving the Lord God glory for what has been done. The prophet will continually be astounded at what the Lord does through him, often while viewing himself as being unworthy of this high calling.

The Lord does not typically anoint those who are full of pride. When He does commission someone who is prideful, He will humble that individual before He brings that person to the fullness of the anointing placed upon him. I believe that is exactly what the Lord did with Joseph.

I want to interject here that as people go through their lives, they may encounter hardship. When these things occur, there are choices to be made. You can be crushed and allow the hardship to dictate and define the rest of your life. You can complain that your life is too hard and unfair blaming God and rebelling against him. The best way to look at hardship in your life is to view it as an opportunity for the Lord to work in your life. I'm not saying that hardship isn't difficult. Believe me, I know it can be very difficult. Having lived through many hardships in my own life has taught me that. What I am saying is that you can take the hardship in your life to the Lord and ask Him how enduring it can bring you closer to Him. You can allow the Lord to use the difficult times you encounter, and the way you endure them to bring glory to the Lord.

One of my favorite portions of scripture says in part, "But we have this treasure in jars of clay to show that this all-surpassing power is from God and not from us. We are hard pressed on every side, but not crushed; perplexed, but not in despair; persecuted, but not abandoned; struck down, but not destroyed. We always carry around in our body the death of Jesus, so that the life of Jesus may also be revealed in our body...Therefore, we do not lose heart. Though outwardly we are wasting away, yet inwardly we are being renewed day by day. For our light and momentary troubles are achieving for us an eternal glory that far outweighs them all. So, we fix our eyes not on what is seen, but on what is unseen, since what is seen is temporary, but what is unseen is eternal." (II Corinthians 4:7-18)

There may be people in the body of Christ today who are called to be prophets but refuse to acknowledge the Lord's call and act upon it. They refuse to spend time in prayer actually being so bold as to ignore the Lord's call instead of responding to him. Remember what Jonah did when the Lord called him?

I encourage those who have been called by the Lord, and anointed to minister in the office of the prophet to step into the call. Do not be afraid of what is ahead. God has called you, and He will equip you to fulfill His purpose for your life.

I was called and commissioned to be a prophet in June of 1979. It was a month before I gave birth to my first son. I had spent hours before the Lord on that day repenting and rededicating my life to Him. We won't be getting into the pile of ashes that I viewed my life to be. As I was raking through the dregs of my life and sincerely repenting before the Lord, He started speaking. He said, "I have forgiven all your sins, and I am now calling you to be My mouthpiece to the body of Christ." I responded by saying, "Who me? Lord, look at all the sinful things I have done. I am so weak in spirit and My flesh is very strong! How can I even think of being Your voice to the body of Christ." He said, "I work through the weak; I will be your strength; trust and obey Me."

The next Sunday in church, as a message in tongues came forth, my heart started pounding like it might come out of my chest. I felt shaking on the inside of my body. As the message in tongues ended, I felt what could only be described as the Lord placing His hands on my shoulders and pressing down with power. I also felt a comforting warmth flowing all over my body. I then heard the Lord say, "Open your mouth and speak as I give you the words." I obeyed and the word came forth. It is something I will never forget!

What I am talking about has an old-fashioned term associated with it; I John 2:20, calls it an unction. A more modern term would be to call it an anointing. These are some of the ways the Holy Spirit gets our attention and confirms that He wants an individual to speak for Him.

Questions for Study and Discussion

1. Once a believer receives his anointing and commission as a prophet, does he always step into the office immediately? Explain.

2. How does the commission to be a prophet come?

3. Is it possible for a prophet of the Lord to be sent to prison and still be a prophet? Explain.

4. When God anoints and appoints someone to be a prophet, what type of person does He choose?

5. What choices does a believer have when he encounters hardship?

CHAPTER 18

PRAYER CAN CHANGE THE MIND OF GOD

When the Lord sends revelation about something terrible that He is about to send on the earth, prophets are drawn by the Holy Spirit to intercede and plead with the Lord to prevent disaster. This type of revelation is often conditional and prayer can change the outcome. God calls His people to pray and intercede for many different reasons. Intercession isn't just for prophets. However, when revelation comes to a prophet, their first response should be to pray and intercede. There will be times the prophet needs to fast along with intense prayer, in an attempt to turn away the Lord's wrath. I want to remind everyone that Jesus sits at the right hand of God the Father making intersession for His people. Jesus also places a burden on His people to intercede for others and for the nations. It is a blessing when the Lord calls us to pray; it builds our faith and blesses the ones for whom we are called to pray.

When the angel of the Lord spoke to Abraham in Genesis 18:16-33 telling him that the Lord was going to destroy the cities of Sodom and Gomorrah, Abraham dared to stand before the Lord, and ask Him to spare these cities where his nephew was living. He did what prophets do; he stood in the gap for those cities asking the Lord if He would sweep away the righteous along with the wicked? While the Lord's mind was not changed in this case, He did make provision for Abraham's nephew to escape this disaster.

Hezekiah, in II Kings 20, became sick, and sent for the prophet Isaiah to go to God and ask if Hezekiah would recover. Isaiah received a word from the Lord saying, "This is what the Lord says, 'Put your house in order, because you are going to die; you will not recover.'" After Isaiah received this word from the Lord and spoke it to the king, Hezekiah prayed to the Lord and reminded God how he had been faithful to the Lord, and served Him wholeheartedly. Hezekiah wept bitterly before the Lord, and humbled himself. As a result of his humility before the Lord and his own intercession, God changed His mind. God spoke to Isaiah and sent him back to Hezekiah to speak a new word to the king. This is the message God spoke through Isaiah, "I have heard your prayer and seen your tears; I will heal you. On the third day from now you will go up to the temple of the Lord. I will add fifteen years to your life." (II Kings 20:5-6)

In this case the prophet spoke a word from the Lord and left the kings presence. Hezekiah interceded for himself, and God changed His mind sending Isaiah back to change the word that he had originally spoken. It is the prophet's obligation to speak the word of the Lord exactly as God speaks it. The prophet must be open for the Lord to change His mind, and send him back to declare a new word from the Lord.

David told Nathan that he wanted to build a house for the Lord. Nathan replied to David, "Whatever you have in mind do it, for God is with you." (I Chronicles 17:2) However, that night the Lord spoke to Nathan contradicting what Nathan had told the king. "But that night the Word of God came to Nathan, saying: 'Go and tell My servant David, this is what the Lord says: You are not the one to build Me a house to dwell in.'" (I Chronicles 4:3-4) The Lord went on to tell David that because he was a man of war and bloodshed it would be his son who succeeded him that would build the house of the Lord.

Questions for Study and Discussion

1. Can revelation given by God be either conditional or unconditional?

2. Was the revelation given to Abraham about the cities of Sodom and Gomorrah be either conditional or unconditional? Explain.

3. When Hezekiah humbled himself before the Lord and wept bitterly before Him, what happened?

4. Does the Lord ever change a word that He has sent a prophet to give to someone? Please explain.

CHAPTER 19

PROPHETS HAVE VARYING LEVELS OF SPIRITUAL POWER

After God called Moses and appointed Aaron to repeat the words that Moses spoke to him, the Lord said the following, "See, I have made you (Moses) like God to Pharaoh, and your brother Aaron will be your prophet." (Exodus 7:1)

You will find in studying the Word of God that there are varying levels of power within those who minister in the office of the prophet. In the above scripture the Lord called Moses to be a mighty and powerful voice for Him. God told Moses he would be as God to Pharaoh. There were many other very powerful prophets like Samuel, Ezekiel, Elijah, Elisha, and Daniel to name a few.

Elijah was known to part waters, and to be transported from place to place by the Holy Spirit. This happened often! Before airplanes, there was Elijah transported by the Holy Spirit from one place to the next. At Elijah's command, all rain in the land stopped for three years. He called fire down from heaven twice, and it consumed a total of 102 men. (II Kings 1:9-15) He was known to raise the dead. Likewise, the prophet Elisha received a double portion of the anointing that was upon Elijah. He parted waters as Elijah had done, and raised the dead through the power of the Holy Spirit. He also performed many other miracles.

There were also prophets, who seemingly had less power as miracle workers, but they were none-the-less prophets; a few of these were Amos, Jonah, Micah, Nahum and Habakkuk. Daniel was considered a powerful prophet by many. He had the ability through the Holy Spirit to interpret dreams. While he was delivered from the lions' den by the hand of God; there are no actual miracles that are recorded having occurred by his hand.

Understand that the function of a prophet is to be the voice of God to the body of Christ. Prophets' lives are used as examples to call attention to the sin and wickedness that is taking place in the world. Each prophet operates differently based on the Lord's commission. Just as the manifestation gifts operate differently in those through whom the Holy Spirit operates; the prophets operate at the Lord's direction and with the level of power that the Holy Spirit places upon them.

Being a prophet is not based on signs and wonders, and one should keep in mind that it is not a competition. It is based upon receiving an anointing and a commission from the Holy Spirit to be an example to the people of God in word and deed. The prophet is the vessel through whom God Himself speaks and works. It is at great cost and with extreme humility that men and women of God willingly step into the office of the prophet. When operating under the anointing and in the office of the prophet, one must die to all they are and allow the Holy Spirit to speak and operate through them. He must get all the glory and honor.

Questions for Study and Discussion

1. What was Moses told by God about his responsibility to Pharaoh?

2. What did God say Aaron's position was to be with regard to Moses?

3. Do all prophets have the same level of power? Explain.

CHAPTER 20

PROPHET AS THE VOICE OF GOD

S tating that the prophet is simply the voice of God is not really adequate when it comes to defining a prophet. We discussed the definition of a prophet that God gave earlier, but we need to go deeper into what being the voice of God really means.

The word of the prophet is used by God as a way to awaken His inattentive people to take action. In essence, God uses His prophets to shake the people of God awake. When God through Jonah preached to the people of Nineveh they, were awakened to their sin and wickedness, and they repented.

The Holy Spirit is unleashed through the manifestation of a prophetic word. In the Book of Jeremiah, we read, "Because the people have spoken these words, I will make My words in your mouth a fire, and these people the wood that it consumes." (Jeremiah 5:14)

The word of the Lord spoken through His prophet will not only awaken the Lord's people; it will light a fire within them motivating them to respond to His word. The Lord will provide guidance and wise counsel to His people through the words His prophets speak. God will also use His prophets to speak correction and to convict His people when they have sinned against Him. The prophet speaks out of obedience. When a prophet speaks correction or conviction, the body of Christ often attacks the prophet instead of going to God for clarity or to repent. It takes a great deal of boldness to be a prophet and speak for the Lord. Often there are consequences for speaking truthfully and obediently what the Lord assigns a prophet to speak. You have heard of shooting the messenger?

In the Book of I Kings, you will find an account of King Ahab asking Jehoshaphat to join with him to attack Ramoth Gilead. Before he committed to go with Ahab, Jehoshaphat asked Ahab if he had sought the counsel of the Lord. Ahab called together 400 prophets for their counsel, but these were not prophets of God. All of these prophets predicted success. Jehoshaphat asked, "Is there no longer a prophet of the Lord here whom we can inquire of?" (I Kings 22:7)

King Ahab told Jehoshaphat there was a prophet, but he never prophesied anything good for Ahab, and he hated him. Nevertheless, Ahab sent for Micaiah the prophet. While those who went to get Micaiah were bringing him to Ahab, they told Micaiah all the other prophets had prophesied that Ahab would be victorious, and they suggested he agree with them; Micaiah responded by telling them he must speak only what the Lord gave him to speak.

Micaiah received a message for Ahab saying, "I saw all Israel scattered on the hills like sheep without a shepherd, and the Lord said, 'These people have no master. Let each one go home in peace.'"… "Therefore, hear the word of the Lord: I saw the Lord sitting on His throne with all the multitudes of heaven standing around Him on His right and on His left. And the Lord said, 'Who will entice Ahab into attacking Ramoth Gilead and going to his death there?' "One suggested this, and another that. Finally, a spirit came forward, stood before the Lord and said, 'I will entice him.' 'By what means?' The Lord asked. 'I will go out and be a deceiving spirit in the mouths of all his prophets,' he said…"So now the Lord has put a deceiving spirit in the mouths of all these prophets of yours. The Lord has decreed disaster for you." (I Kings 22:17-23)

As a result of his obedience to the Lord, Micaiah was slapped in the face by Zedekiah, and Ahab ordered Micaiah be imprisoned receiving nothing but bread and water to eat until Ahab returned from the battle. Micaiah's response to his punishment was to say, "If you ever return safely, the Lord has not spoken through me." (I Kings 22:28) Can't you just picture Micaiah speaking that parting shot as they were dragging him out of Ahab's presence? But what Micaiah spoke was proven true. Ahab died in the battle, and the word the Lord had spoken through Micaiah was confirmed on that day.

I want to point out, though Jehoshaphat required Ahab to seek counsel from a prophet of God, when the word of the Lord came forth telling Ahab he would be defeated in battle, Jehoshaphat still went into battle with Ahab in spite of the word the Lord had spoken. Jehoshaphat also seemingly ignored the treatment of the prophet when he was slapped and imprisoned for speaking the word the Lord had given.

There are many examples of the penalty prophets can face for being obedient to the Lord. Another example of this is found in Zechariah. "This is what God says: 'Why do you disobey the Lord's commands? You will not prosper. Because you have forsaken the Lord, He has forsaken you.' But they plotted against him, and by order of the king they stoned him to death in the courtyard of the Lord's temple." (II Chronicles 24:20-21)

The words a prophet speaks, though from the Lord, are often rejected. When this happens the prophet sometimes takes that rejection upon himself when, in fact, it is really God who is being rejected. It takes maturity for the prophet to recognize this truth and not take it personally. It takes dedication and trust in the Lord to accept any punishment that might result from being obedient to the Lord as well.

The prophet must seek the Lord's counsel on behalf of the body of Christ and the nation. He waits to hear the word of the Lord as he asks Him for guidance, direction, encouragement and even rebuke. God may not always give a word, but it is the obligation of the prophet to seek the word of the Lord continually and to accurately speak the message God gives. In fact, much of the work the prophet does is done in the privacy of his prayer closet. Prophets spend a great deal of time praying and interceding for the body of Christ.

The scripture says that no man can prophesy unless the Holy Spirit works in him, but a true prophet can arouse or call into action the gift that has been given to him. Paul urges Timothy to "stir up" the gift he has been given. (II Timothy 1:6) This is an essential function of a prophet. When the people of God need counsel from the Lord, they can go to the prophet. The prophet through the use of worship music, prayer and fasting, or simply sitting in the awareness of the Lord's presence can ask for guidance or direction on behalf of the Lord's people.

As a prophet, I spend a great deal of time seeking the Lord and listening for Him to speak messages for the body of Christ. I feel it is my responsibility to be ready in spirit so that when the Lord wants to give a word, or minister to the body in some way I am ready to receive and speak for Him. This is the way it should be with all prophets. It requires setting aside time to sit before Him, allowing Him to make Himself known. He is my confidant. I speak my heart to Him, and He speaks His heart to me. It is a sweet time of fellowship.

Another significant aspect of the office of the prophet is the power of the Holy Spirit that is bestowed to those who serve as prophets. Prophets are God's friends. To operate under the full anointing of the office, a prophet must be pure and clean, and he must reverence God.

One who has been commissioned to be a prophet will regularly minister through prophecy. Their prophetic words will mature over time to include words of knowledge, words of wisdom (revelation), words of correction or admonition, conviction, guidance, and counsel in addition to exhortation, edification, and comfort.

A prophet speaking a word of prophecy will speak with an anointing and power that comes only from the Holy Spirit. Someone speaking simple prophecy for edification, exhortation, or comfort will not speak with the same power and authority that a prophet will have when speaking.

Questions for Study and Discussion

1. To what did the Lord compare His words in the mouth of the prophet in Jeremiah 5:14?

2. What did God say about the people of Israel at that time?

3. When a prophet speaks correction or conviction to the body of Christ what is likely to happen?

4. What was Ahab required to do before Jehoshaphat would join with him to attack Ramoth Gilead?

5. Ahab hated the prophet Micaiah. Why?

6. As a result of being obedient to the Lord, what happened to Micaiah?

7. What was Micaiah's response to Ahab when he rejected the word he had spoken?

8. Did Jehoshaphat join Ahab in battle? What was the outcome of the battle?

9. What happened to Zechariah for being obedient to the Lord?

10. To operate under the full anointing of the office, a prophet must be what?

11. Prophecy spoken by a prophet will mature over time to include what?

CHAPTER 21

PROPHETS – OLD TESTAMENT VERSES NEW TESTAMENT

There are differences between the prophets in the Old and New Testaments. These differences are due to a change in the relationship God has with His people.

The Old Testament prophet was unique because of the Holy Spirit's operation in him. The Holy Spirit was not resident within the prophets at that time. He was not resident within anyone except Jesus until the baptism of the Holy Spirit occurred in Acts, Chapter 2. All of the manifestation gifts of the Holy Spirit were available in the Old Testament except the gift of speaking in tongues and the gift of interpretation of tongues as has been mentioned previously. These two gifts did not appear until the Day of Pentecost when the baptism of the Holy Spirit was given.

When the Lord gave a message to an Old Testament prophet, the Holy Spirit would rest upon him. Once the message was given, the Spirit would lift from the prophet. The people of God did not communicate with God directly in the Old Testament. The prophet in the Old Testament operated as a mediator between God and man.

The people of Israel actually asked God not to appear to them or speak to them. The reason for this is found in the Book of Deuteronomy. The people of Israel said, "Let us not hear the voice of the Lord our God nor see this great fire anymore, or we will die." (Deuteronomy

18:16) God complied with their request and said, "I will raise up for them a prophet like you (Moses) from among their fellow Israelites, and I will put my words in his mouth." (Deuteronomy 18:18) God had spoken to the people of Israel and it scared them so badly they asked Him not to speak directly to them anymore; they preferred to have a mediator.

In the New Testament, all of God's people have the infilling of the Holy Spirit available to them. This means individual believers have the ability to communicate directly with God. I say that all of the Lord's people have the Holy Spirit available to them, but many do not want to experience His infilling. This may be out of fear or lack of understanding of how the Holy Spirit operates. Personally, I want all that is available from God. His Holy Spirit is part of the Godhead, and He is available to reside within all believers of Jesus Christ. He does not force Himself upon His people; we must receive Him willingly.

In Matthew 27:51, scripture says that when Jesus died, the veil in the temple was torn from top to bottom. This gave everyone access to go into the holy of holies where they could stand in the presence of the Lord.

In the New Testament, a mediator is no longer required for God's people to communicate with Him. Any believer through prayer and meditation can communicate with God. Understand that when a mediator is needed, the true mediator for the people of God is Jesus Christ. In other words, Jesus is the true prophet. The English Standard Version of the Bible says it this way, "For the testimony of Jesus is the spirit of prophecy." (Revelation 19:10) Those who have been anointed and commissioned as prophets of God are the vessels used by the Lord to speak to the body of Christ. The prophet is still the voice of the Lord to the body of Christ, and his life is an example to the people of God. The requirement that a prophet come against sin when he sees it, or be held accountable to the Lord is still in place.

Though it is possible for all believers to hear the voice of the Lord, most of us do not hear God speaking to us personally. There are many reasons for this; believers today are not always attentive to the voice of the Lord. We are often too busy with our own personal problems, our responsibilities at work, or raising our families to pay attention to what the Holy Spirit is speaking. Something else that controls our lives is technology; often to our detriment. People today can't even seem to walk down a sidewalk or drive their car without talking on their cell phone, texting, or reading and inputting to social media. We are too easily distracted and don't spend the time we need to spend with the Lord to be able to hear clearly and directly.

In the New Testament God places an anointing within His prophets and a commission upon them to speak God's word to the people of the Lord. Often this is the only way the Holy Spirit can get through to His people. It is through the voice of the prophet that the Lord's people are stirred to action.

The words the prophet speaks are intended to focus their attention on what the Lord wants them to do. It motivates the body of Christ to respond to the Lord as the word comes forth in a public setting.

When a prophet speaks, the Holy Spirit is at work in the one speaking and in those hearing the word of the Lord. As a prophet speaks the power of God is activated and things happen.

"As the rain and the snow come down from heaven, and do not return to it without watering the earth and making it bud and flourish, so that it yields seed for the sower and bread for the eater, so is my word that goes out from my mouth: It will not return to me empty, but will accomplish what I desire and achieve the purpose for which I sent it." (Isaiah 55:10-11)

While anyone who knows the Lord's word can speak a word of edification, exhortation, or comfort, (I Corinthians14:3) a prophet speaking will often include words that convict and admonish a nation, a state, a city, and the believer to repent. God will speak through the prophet when the Lord's people do wrong. The Lord provides a way of escape by speaking through His prophets.

"And your ears will hear a word behind you, 'This is the way, walk in it.'" (Isaiah 30:21, NAS) This scripture describes the way the Holy Spirit speaks individually to believers to prompt them that what they are about to do is sinful or against God's will. I believe that each human has implanted within them a basic understanding of right and wrong; unless there is a mental disorder that prevents them from determining right from wrong. I believe this scripture is actually describing the human conscience that is directed by the Holy Spirit. Of course, a conscience is only effective if the Lord's people will listen, and change what they intended to do. Human beings can ignore their conscience, and the consequences of that can result in separation from God.

When a prophet speaks a prophetic word publicly, it can often function in the church as a source to inspire the body of Christ to act instead of them simply hearing a message.

We find a demonstration in I Chronicles where it says in part, "David, together with the commanders of the army, set apart some of the sons of Asaph, Heman and Jeduthun for the ministry of prophesying accompanied by harps, lyres and cymbals." (I Chronicles 25:1-3)

I have come across people throughout the time I have ministered in the office of the prophet who want to be prophets. They look at being a prophet as being somehow glamorous and special. Understand that ministering in the office of the prophet is a humbling and very difficult call that comes from God. I have spoken about some of the suffering that prophets of old experienced. It was and is very difficult to obey the call and anointing to minister in the office of the prophet. No one should seek to be called as a prophet of God. Likewise, no one should say "No" if called to this important office.

In studying scripture, you will find that prophets in the Old Testament were not popular. When a prophet spoke the word of the Lord to kings, it often prompted the king to want to kill him. Prophets were sometimes jailed and killed in the Old Testament for speaking the Lord's word as we have already established in this study. In spite of this you will also see that it was the prophet of God the pharaoh or king called when someone was needed to interpret a troubling dream or vision, or when they wanted to inquire of the Lord for direction.

You don't see world leaders calling for the prophets now days to ask the Lord for direction, at least this is not something that is publicized. Even the mere suggestion that a world leader ask the Lord for His counsel would most likely bring sarcasm, criticism, and it would call into question a leader's soundness of mind. In the past history of this nation, several presidents or their wives sought counsel from false prophets who were trying to see into the future.

The Old Testament prophets spoke judgment through the prophetic word. A good example of this is found in Jeremiah where God through the prophet says, "Therefore this is what the Lord says: 'I'm about to remove you from the face of the earth. This very year you are going to die, because you have preached rebellion against the Lord.'" (Jeremiah 28:16)

The prophets of God in the Old Testament were known to carry out the will of God when the people of Israel were unwilling to do so. Samuel actually killed Agag, king of the Amalekites because King Saul disobeyed God and let him live. This is recorded in I Samuel 15:33.

Elijah in I Kings 18:19 told Ahab, "Now summon the people from all over Israel to meet me on Mount Carmel. And bring the 450 prophets of Baal and the 400 prophets of Asherah, who eat at Jezebel's table." When they were gathered, Elijah challenged the prophets of Baal to make an offering to their god and he would do the same and offer his sacrifice to the Lord. After the prophets of Baal prepared their sacrifice and prayed to their god for a long time with no success; Elijah offered his sacrifice and God accepted his sacrifice, and He sent fire from heaven that consumed not only the sacrifice, but the altar on which his sacrifice had been offered. Elijah then had the prophets of Baal brought to the Kishon Valley and slaughtered there. I don't believe Elijah was the only one slaughtering the prophets of Baal as I have heard some teach. I believe the army of Israel helped with that task.

In the many times I have heard this incident taught, I have never heard anyone speak about the 400 prophets of Asherah that are mentioned as being in attendance. Scripture only says those prophets were present when the sacrifices were offered. It does not mention those prophets when it comes to the slaughter. We do not know if those prophets were slain as well. We do know that the 450 prophets who represented Baal were slaughtered that day.

I want you to realize that there were 850 prophets present, representing two different gods, when the Lord sent fire from heaven that devoured the offering Elijah offered. Perhaps the prophets of Asherah were just observers who then went away testifying of what happened. Let me be clear. Scripture does not say this, it is just a suggestion as to what might have happened.

There is no record in the New Testament where God sent a prophet to kill someone who had been disobedient to the Lord. Certainly, today there would be a high price to pay for doing something like that. In fact, the Lord would not do that in this current day. Jesus sacrificed Himself for our redemption ushering us into a period of grace that continues to this day. He pours His mercy out upon us who will receive Him instead of us having to face His wrath.

God demanded absolute obedience from His chosen ones. In the Old Testament you find many of the prophets doing strange things. Isaiah walked around naked for three years (Isaiah 20:4). Ezekiel was told to shave his head bald with a sword. (Ezekiel 5:1) He was also told by God that his wife (the love of his life) was going to die, and he was not to mourn for her. (Ezekiel 24:17) Hosea was told to marry a prostitute. (Hosea 1:2) We do not see things like this happening today, but they were done enough in the Old Testament that prophets were often considered to be strange. If you study the scriptures, you will find many more examples.

Prophets were known to speak guidance to the followers of the Lord. In the Book of Acts, the Lord provided revelation through Agabus the prophet, "During this time some prophets came down from Jerusalem to Antioch. One of them, named Agabus, stood up and through the Spirit, predicted that a severe famine would spread over the entire Roman world." (Acts 11:27-28) It was through this revelation that the disciples were able to help provide for the needs of the body of Christ in Judah during this famine.

There are times when a scripture can have more than one meaning. The scripture below is one such instance. This passage is the record of how Peter knew he was being sent to preach to the Gentiles.

"About noon the following day as they were on their journey and approaching the city, Peter went up on the roof to pray. He became hungry and wanted something to eat, and while the meal was being prepared, he fell into a trance. He saw heaven opened and something like a large sheet being let down to earth by its four corners. It contained all kinds of four-footed animals, as well as reptiles and birds. Then a voice told him, 'Get up, Peter, kill and eat.' Surely not, Lord! 'Peter replied.' I have never eaten anything impure or unclean. The voice spoke to him a second time, 'Do not call anything impure that God has made clean.' This happened three times, and immediately the sheet was taken back to heaven...While Peter was still thinking about the vision, the Spirit said to him, 'Simon, three men are looking for you. So, get up and go downstairs. Do not hesitate to go with them, for I have sent them.'" (Acts 10:9-16)

In this scripture God is telling Peter that the Word of God is now available to all mankind, not just the Jews. God actually sent people to invite him to preach to the Gentiles. I believe there is also a second purpose for this scripture. The Lord is also reminding Peter that the restrictions on eating certain foods had been lifted. These restrictions were part of the ceremonial laws that were done away with when Jesus, the Son of God was sent to the earth.

As you know, there were many laws in the Old Testament related to restricting the consumption of various living creatures. In the New Testament the Lord's people still abided by those restrictions though they had been lifted. I refer to Mark where Jesus is teaching, "Don't you see that nothing that enters a person from the outside can defile them? For it doesn't go into their heart but into their stomach, and then out of the body. (In saying this, Jesus declared all foods clean.)" (Mark 7:18-19)

Through this vision, the Lord was reminding Peter those restrictions were no longer in place. Peter told the Lord that he had never eaten anything impure or unclean, indicating he was still restricting himself from eating foods considered unclean. If Peter had gone to the Gentiles and held them to the restrictions formerly in place, it might have prevented them from fully embracing the teachings offering them salvation. Let the reader be aware, that many in the body of Christ today try to place all kinds of restrictions on how believers are to live their lives. Jesus made it clear that we are to love God and our neighbor. I don't believe He cares about many of the restrictions people want to put on their fellow believers.

Paul also received a word from the Lord through the prophets that sent him to the Gentiles to preach the gospel of Christ. This is the second scripture that confirms the promises of God were now available to more than just the Jews. It is as follows: "Which was not made known to people in other generations as it has now been revealed by the Spirit to God's holy apostles and prophets. This mystery is that through the gospel, the Gentiles are heirs together with Israel, members together of one body, and sharers together in the promise in Christ Jesus." (Ephesians 3:5-6)

In the Old Testament, the Lord's chosen people were the Jews and only the Jews. In the New Testament after Christ was crucified, raised from the dead, and ascended into heaven, the word of the Lord that brings salvation became available to all people both Jews and Gentiles.

Another rather big difference between the prophets in the Old Testament and the New is this. In the Old Testament when a prophet spoke with less than complete accuracy, it brought that prophet into judgment.

"If a prophet, or one who foretells by dreams, appears among you and announces to you a sign or wonder, and if the sign or wonder spoken of takes place, and the prophet says, 'Let us follow other gods and let us worship them,' you must not listen to the words of that prophet or dreamer…It is the Lord your God you must follow, and Him you must revere. Keep His commands and obey Him; serve Him and hold fast to Him. That prophet or dreamer must be put to death for inciting rebellion against the Lord your God." (Deuteronomy 13:1-5)

"But a prophet who presumes to speak in My name anything I have not commanded, or a prophet who speaks in the name of other gods, is to be put to death. You may say to yourselves, 'How can we know when a message has not been spoken by the Lord?' If what a prophet proclaims in the name of the Lord does not take place or come true, that is a message the Lord has not spoken. That prophet has spoken presumptuously, so do not be alarmed." (Deuteronomy 18:20-22)

In the New Testament the Holy Spirit was made available to all God's people and with that, some changes occurred. Prophets are no longer killed for making a mistake when speaking revelation. Errors can occur especially when one is learning to hear the voice of the Lord and to speak revelation. Although all prophetic revelation comes from God, New Testament prophets are flawed and can make mistakes. When this happens, it is best to acknowledge the mistake, learn from it, and ask God's forgiveness. The prophet's responsibility is to seek the Lord for confirmation when revelation is received. The scripture says that prophecy must be judged by the prophets to determine what is good and what is evil.

I have seen people who wanted to prophesy so badly they have gotten up in a service and proclaimed a word that was not given by the Lord. In the Old Testament they would have been put to death. We serve a merciful God who does not strike people dead because they are over-zealous or make a mistake. Recognize God knows the motivation that is in their hearts. He will deal with the one who is trying to deceive the body of Christ.

Most of the time when I receive a message from the Lord I pray over that word and ask the Lord to remove anything that is not from Him. I say most of the time, because there are times when I receive spontaneous words that must be given when the anointing is there to give the word. However, after many years of maturing in this ministry, I will recognize quickly if something I am hearing is not scriptural. All prophets speak through faith that what we are saying is from God. He will confirm the words of a true prophet of God.

In Acts 21:10-11, Agabus the prophet gave a word of revelation to Paul warning that if he went up to Jerusalem, the Jews would bind him in the same way he had bound himself in front of Paul. The prophecy was accepted even though it was not completely accurate. It was not the Jews who bound Paul, but the Romans. Some might try to explain this away by saying that the Jews initiated this event, but the word was specific that the Jews would bind Paul. It was partially wrong.

In the body of Christ today, when someone speaks a revelation that predicts something that does not happen, it is viewed more as a mistake. If the same person continues to speak revelation predicting things that do not happen, it is evidence that the revelation is in error, and this person should not be allowed to speak to the body of Christ because he has lost credibility. This is something that the leadership of the church will determine.

If someone in the body of Christ declares that the Lord is coming back for His church on a specific date, beware. The Word of God says, "Watch therefore, for ye know neither the day nor the hour wherein the Son of man cometh." (Matthew 25:13, KJV) Several times over the years well-known preachers and evangelists have predicted the Lord will return on a specific date. I don't know why they do that because it is strictly against scripture. At that point these pastors and evangelists cannot be viewed as credible. I have actually seen times when the prediction did not come to pass, and the one who gave the date in the first place "corrected the date" and went on preaching that the world is going to end on a new date. By doing this you can be sure that the predictor is mistaken, and he should not be given any creditability.

You must also keep in mind that some revelation is conditional. If a conditional revelation is spoken to the people, prayer can change the outcome. That means what was spoken may not take place because prayer changed God's mind. Sometimes certain things must occur before a conditional word of revelation can take place.

Because of errors that have occurred, many churches who once welcomed the operation of the manifestation gifts of the Holy Spirit, have stopped seeking the Lord's word for the body of Christ. When a message is actually sent by the Lord, often that word is met with skepticism. Scripture says, "Do not treat prophecies with contempt but test them all; hold on to what is good, reject every kind of evil." (I Thessalonians 5:20-22)

Questions for Study and Discussion

1. Which manifestation gifts do not appear in the Old Testament?

2. What would the Holy Spirit do when He wanted a prophet in the Old Testament to say or do something?

3. Why did the Lord's people ask God not to speak to them in the Old Testament?

4. The prophets in the Old Testament became what for God?

5. In the New Testament and even today, the people of God have what available to them?

6. Who is the true prophet of God?

7. How can believers communicate with God today?

8. Why don't people today seem to hear the voice of the Lord?

9. What did the prophet Isaiah say about the word of the Lord?

10. What does scripture say the Holy Spirit does to prompt His people that what they are doing is wrong?

11. How did the prophets of God respond in the Old Testament when the will of God was not carried out? Give some examples.

12. The Lord's chosen people in the Old Testament were who?

13. When did salvation become available to all people?

14. In the Old Testament when a prophet spoke with less than complete accuracy, what happened?

15. In the New Testament and today are prophets who are not completely accurate put to death? Explain.

16. What should a prophet now days do if His revelation is inaccurate?

17. Who is to judge prophecy?

18. Is there a record in the New Testament of a prophecy that was less than accurate? Explain.

19. When is it acceptable for revelation not to occur as it has been prophesied?

CHAPTER 22

GOD'S PROPHETS CAN SPEAK THEIR MIND TO THE LORD

From the very beginning of the relationship between God and Moses he spoke His mind to God. When God called Moses to be His voice to the people of Israel and to Pharaoh, Moses suggested that He look elsewhere. Moses told God that he did not speak well; in fact, he was a stutterer. When God assured Moses, he was His chosen one, Moses asked God to send someone who could speak for him. God complied with this request by anointing Aaron to speak for him.

As time went by, the people of Israel started complaining against God. They grew tired of the manna that the Lord was providing daily, and they began to demand meat. Moses went to God, and this is what he said to God.

"Why have you brought this trouble on your servant? What have I done to displease you that you put the burden of all these people on me? Did I conceive all these people? Did I give them birth? Why do you tell me to carry them in my arms, as a nurse carries an infant, to the land you promised on oath to their ancestors? Where can I get meat for all these people? They keep wailing to me, 'Give us meat to eat!' I cannot carry all these people by myself; the burden is too heavy for me. If this is how you are going to treat me, please go ahead and kill me, if I have found favor in your eyes, and do not let me face my own ruin." (Numbers 11:11-15) Notice the words, "Please go ahead and kill me, if I have found favor in your eyes."

What a polite way to ask God to strike you dead! Do you suppose Moses really meant for the Lord to kill him? I doubt it, after all he was speaking out of frustration, and the Lord answered the cry of his heart not the words he spoke.

This was God's prophet complaining that the task God had called him to do was too much for him to handle on his own. God did not get angry with Moses; He heard his cry.

"Bring me 70 of Israel's elders who are known to you as leaders and officials among the people. Have them come to the tent of meeting that they may stand there with you. I will come down and speak with you there, and I will take some of the power of the Spirit that is on you and put it on them. They will share the burden of the people with you so that you will not have to carry it alone…Then the Lord came down in the cloud and spoke with him, and He took some of the power of the Spirit that was on Moses and put it on the 70 elders. When the Spirit rested on them, they prophesied—but did not do so again." (Numbers 11:16-30)

The anointing was so strong that even two elders who had not joined the others at the tent of meeting began to prophesy in the camp. When it was suggested that these two men should be stopped from prophesying, Moses replied, "Are you jealous for my sake? I wish that all the Lord's people were prophets and that the Lord would put His Spirit on them." (Numbers 11:29)

This was a demonstration of the humility that Moses had before the Lord and the people. He didn't care who was anointed by God to prophesy just so the Lord sent him help. We should all have that kind of an attitude when it comes to the work of the Lord. These 70 elders were not prophets, this was the manifestation gift of prophesy that the Lord bestowed upon these elders, and it was only to show that God was setting these men apart to assist Moses. The scripture says, they did not prophesy again. God heard Moses when he cried out in frustration. He responded to the cry of his heart, and not the words that he spoke.

It is hard to fathom the strength of the power that was upon Moses. Can you imagine? God took just some of the power that was upon Moses and placed it upon the 70 elders. The portion of power that was taken from Moses and placed upon the elders, was so strong it prompted all those elders to spontaneously prophesy. Yet, there was still enough power left upon Moses, that he was still a very powerful voice for the Lord. He continued to perform mighty miracles even after some of His power was taken and placed upon the elders of Israel.

When Jezebel found out Elijah had put all the prophets of Baal to death, she sought to have him killed. What did Elijah do? Mighty and powerful prophet that he was, he ran for his life! Scripture says, "Elijah was afraid and ran for his life. When he came to Beersheba in Judah, he left his servant there, while he went a day's journey into the wilderness. He came to a broom bush, sat down under it and prayed that he might die. 'I have had enough, Lord,' he said. 'Take my life; I am no better than my ancestors.'" (I Kings 19:34)

Jonah became angry with God for sparing the city of Nineveh. Jonah said the following to the Almighty God, "Isn't this what I said, Lord, when I was still at home? That is what I tried to forestall by fleeing to Tarshish. I knew that you are a gracious and compassionate God, slow to anger and abounding in love, a God who relents from sending calamity. Now, Lord, take away my life for it is better for me to die than to live." (Jonah 4:2-3) He was basically throwing a temper tantrum because God chose to spare Nineveh. Remember that Jonah had been punished by God for running from His call to go to Nineveh in the first place. He spent several days in the belly of a large fish for his disobedience to God. He was required by God to go and preach to those people when he believed all along that God would spare them.

Perhaps he believed God was treating him unfairly. Perhaps he was concerned that people would view him as a false prophet because the city was not overthrown as he had prophesied. Talk about extreme venting! Again, Jonah said to God, "It would be better for me to die than to live." (Jonah 4:8) God asked Jonah if it was appropriate for him to be angry. Jonah is talking directly to God when he again says,

"And I'm so angry I wish I were dead." (Jonah 4:9) Three times in this chapter Jonah told God he wished he were dead.

How did God respond? God explained that there were 120,000 people in Nineveh, and He asked Jonah if He shouldn't be concerned for them as well as the animals living there. God could have killed Jonah in this instance, but even as God cared for the 120,000 people of Nineveh, He also cared for Jonah. He was very bold to speak to God out of so much anger, but God did not kill him, He comforted Jonah and restored him.

As you see, three of God's prophets asked God to put them to death because of the burden placed upon them by being obedient to the voice of God. Prophets as messengers of God can be overwhelmed at times. God allows His prophets to come to Him and express themselves in ways that the ordinary believer might not be bold enough to do. Rest assured, when you get frustrated enough with your life and the responsibilities placed upon you by God, you can go to Him and vent. Even though you may ask Him to put you to death with your words, He will hear your heart's cry, and He will respond appropriately. You can see when the prophets came to the point of asking God to put them to death, God reached out with mercy and grace. He ministered to them and restored them through the Spirit of the Lord.

For the prophet, God is their confidant; He is the one who restores them after a fierce battle. He has a powerful connection to His prophets. When prophets are obedient, He stands with them and backs them with all the forces of Heaven.

Questions for Study and Discussion

1. What did Moses do when the people of Israel came to him complaining about how the Lord was treating them? What was God's response?

2. What help did the Lord send Moses in response to his plea to the Lord for help?

3. The Lord anointed 70 elders and set them apart by doing what?

4. What was the evidence that these elders had been anointed by the Lord to help carry the burden so that Moses did not have to carry it alone?

5. When the Lord placed a small portion of the Spirit upon the elders, did they become prophets of God?

6. How did Moses respond when the people wanted to make the two elders stop prophesying in the camp?

7. How did Elijah respond when Jezebel threatened his life?

CHAPTER 23

EXPERIENCED PROPHETS MENTOR NEWER PROPHETS

God, through His Holy Spirit, will teach those He has anointed how to effectively operate as prophets. In doing so, He will speak directly to His messengers giving them direction in what they are to say and do. However, He also uses more experienced prophets to mentor or teach the newer ones. It is important for every believer to have a mentor that can strengthen them in their walk with the Lord. For a prophet of God, having a mentor is vital. If you have been called and anointed by God to be His spokesmen, I encourage you to seek the Lord, and ask Him to place you under the mentorship of an experienced prophet. God will place the new prophet under proven men and women who have functioned in the office of the prophet for many years. These mentors will instruct the new prophet how to effectively minister in this office. This requires the prophet to accept the guidance and teaching of the older and more experienced prophet. Don't get offended when your mentor corrects something you have done or said. There are several examples of experienced prophets teaching and mentoring newer prophets throughout the scriptures.

Let's go back and talk about Moses. When the Lord called Moses to act as His prophet, the first thing Moses did was suggest someone else for this assignment. When God refused His request, Moses then asked God to provide someone who could speak for him. God agreed and placed an anointing upon Aaron to be the spokesman for Moses. Aaron was taught by Moses how to do this. Moses anointed Aaron as priest at the Lord's direction, but He also taught him how to operate in the office of the prophet. God assisted in this process by calling out Aaron and Miriam when they became so proud they thought they could judge Moses concerning his choice of wives. In this lesson, Aaron and Miriam understood that Moses was the one chosen by God, and that they were his helpers. They learned to honor and respect Moses that day, and they learned to reverence the Lord. I refer you to Numbers 12.

One of Moses's teachings was particularly harsh, but it was harsh because of the extreme violation of God's will and word that Aaron committed. While Moses was on Mount Sinai receiving the 10 commandments from God in Exodus 32, the people of Israel grew impatient and asked Aaron to make them a God. Because of his lack of faith in God, and his lack of knowledge of God's will, he told the people to bring him gold items that he then melted and turned into a calf for the people to worship. This was a tremendous violation of what the Lord wanted for the people of Israel. When Moses came down from the mount and found what Aaron had done, he punished the people who worshipped the idol and also Aaron who had made it. He did this by grinding the golden idol into a fine powder and throwing it in their water supply. By doing this, when people drank the water, they had to drink the gold powder as well. This caused a physical purging and cleansing of their bodies. That gold powder would have stayed in that water for many days. It would have been like taking a laxative each time they drank the water. In essence drinking the gold powder was a method of cleansing them of sin from the inside out. Rest assured Aaron did not commit a violation such as this again.

Eli mentored Samuel as the boy was growing up even recognizing the Lord was speaking to him in I Samuel 3:8, and teaching him how to respond when the Lord spoke. The first time the Lord spoke to Samuel was to give him a message concerning his mentor. Eli had lost favor with the Lord, but the Lord still used him to teach and instruct the boy as he grew and entered into the full office as a prophet of God. If you read the scriptural account of Samuel the prophet, you will see that the Lord used the student (Samuel) to prophecy to the teacher (Eli) in I Samuel 3:18.

When the Lord speaks to His prophets, they have an obligation to be obedient and speak every word that has been given with no apology and without fear of consequences. Samuel prophesied to Eli about the judgment of the Lord that had come upon his family because of disobedience. It must have been a very difficult word to give as a young prophet. It needs to be noted that when Samuel spoke the message to Eli, he could have humbled himself and repented before God, but the scripture does not say anything about that happening. Repenting might well have saved Eli from God's judgment upon him and his house.

Samuel mentored and taught Saul and David. Saul rejected Samuel's mentoring. He became prideful, and took it upon himself to ignore the instruction Samuel gave him. You can read Samuel's harsh word to Saul where it says, "You have done a foolish thing," Samuel said, "You have not kept the command the Lord your God gave you; if you had, He would have established your kingdom over Israel for all time. But now your kingdom will not endure; the Lord has sought out a man after His own heart and appointed him ruler of His people because you have not kept the Lord's command." (I Samuel 13:13-14) Giving this word to King Saul brought great distressed to Samuel. Saul's disobedience to God's commands broke Samuel's heart. To see how Saul had become so proud and rebellious against the Lord actually caused Samuel to become depressed.

As a result of Saul's rebellion Samuel was directed by the Lord to place the anointing upon David. There was a great difference between David and Saul. David reverenced the Lord and recognized that it was the power of the Lord upon him that made him strong. He so reverenced the anointing that he would not lay a hand upon Saul to kill him. He patiently waited on the Lord and would not take Saul's life even when it would have been easy to do so.

Elijah mentored Elisha. In I Kings 19:19, God had Elijah place the call to minister as prophet upon Elisha. He was taught by him for many years. Because Elisha walked closely with Elijah and was taught the power of the anointing and the ways of the Lord, Elisha became an even more powerful prophet of God than Elijah. Elisha in turn became a mentor to Gehazi. However, Gehazi rebelled against the Lord, and through a word of knowledge to Elisha that revealed his rebellion, Gehazi became a leper.

In the New Testament you see Jesus mentoring His disciples. Mentoring consists of simply teaching through word and deed. It is also encouraging and counseling when needed. The disciples sat under Jesus's teaching daily. He built and strengthened their faith in God. He taught them the power of God that was theirs. Jesus taught the disciples about the importance of humility, and how harmful pride could be. He showed them miracles and healings, and He taught them that they had the ability through faith in God to perform these wonders just as they saw Him doing.

After Jesus's death the disciples and apostles mentored the churches throughout the world. They traveled through the world as they knew it, teaching and preaching the truth of Jesus. They also sent out disciples to teach and preach the good news that Jesus was the Messiah. The New Testament contains letters, many of which were written by Paul, that were intended to mentor the body of Christ. These letters are filled with teaching about how the people of God were to live. In these letters you will see that not only did the authors teach the ways of the Lord, but they also released the people of God from the legalism and condemnation that had been so prolific in the Old Testament.

The Apostle Paul mentored those traveling with him to various churches. Scripture says these men were helpers. Some of these helpers were Barnabas, Timothy, and Silas. Many of the letters that appear in the New Testament were written to various churches and specific individuals who were serving the Lord. They were filled with teachings that helped to establish how the followers of Christ were to live. In Acts 15:37, you can find the account of Barnabas and Paul having a sharp disagreement concerning who they should take with them as helpers. Barnabas wanted to take Mark, but Paul had lost confidence in him, so the two parted ways. Barnabas took Mark and went to Cyprus, but Paul chose Silas and they went to Syria and Cilicia.

I point this out so you recognize that you will not always agree with other men and women of God. There will be times that the Lord may separate you from those you have respected and been mentored by. God uses these situations to strengthen His prophets and motivate them to step out in faith. If something like this happens in your life, go in love and without resentment or anger. Understand the Lord uses discomfort and sometimes disagreement to help His prophets mature. Stay close to the Lord and seek His guidance in situations like this. When the Lord's people get too comfortable in a place, they often become stagnant. God will stir the waters to cause you to grow. Remember it's not about your comfort; rather, it is about what God needs. It is about obedience to God's call and direction.

Paul's letter to the Romans was filled with explicit instruction on right and wrong. In Romans, Chapter 1, Paul explains how the Roman church claimed to be wise but were actually fools exchanging the immortal God for images made by man to worship instead; thus, becoming idolaters. This idolatry led the Romans to engage in all sorts of depravity and sin.

"Therefore, God gave them over in the sinful desires of their hearts to sexual impurity for the degrading of their bodies with one another. They exchanged the truth about God for a lie, and worshiped and served created things rather than the Creator—who is forever praised. Amen. Because of this, God gave them over to shameful lusts. Even their women exchanged natural sexual relations for unnatural ones. In the same way the men also abandoned natural relations with women and were inflamed with lust for one another. Men committed shameful acts with other men, and received in themselves the due penalty for their error. Furthermore, just as they did not think it worthwhile to retain the knowledge of God, so God gave them over to a depraved mind, so that they do what ought not to be done. They have become filled with every kind of wickedness, evil, greed and depravity. They are full of envy, murder, strife, deceit and malice. They are gossips, slanders, Godhaters, insolent, arrogant and boastful; they invent ways of doing evil; they disobey their parents;

they have no understanding, no fidelity, no love, no mercy. Although they know God's righteous decree that those who do such things deserve death, they not only continue to do these very things but also approve of those who practice them." (Romans 1:24-32) Doesn't this sound like what is going on in our world today? Now, we know why these things happen!

Paul mentored the Jewish community as well as the Gentiles. He taught them the way to the Savior and how to live as righteous people of God. In essence he was emphasizing and teaching God's moral code.

The Apostle Peter was a great mentor for the body, of Christ. He had been humbled by turning his back on Jesus and denying Him just as Jesus had prophesied he would. After a time of repentance, the Lord used Peter in very powerful ways to teach the Jewish and Gentile communities the truth of Jesus Christ.

Through the letters of I and II Peter, the Apostle Peter gave guidance and mentorship to the church of Jesus Christ in Rome and the outlying areas of Rome. His letters are uplifting, encouraging the people to be holy. Peter reminds them to stay pure and to abstain from sinful desires, to live Godly lives. He encourages them to live as examples to the pagans. He reminds the people of God that suffering for the Lord will bring blessing. Peter taught the believers that the Lord will return, and they need to keep themselves blameless before God.

James, the brother of Jesus, became a leader in the church at Jerusalem after Jesus was raised from the dead. He wrote the letter of James, and through it we can see his mentorship to the Jewish and Roman communities.

The Apostle John also mentored the people of God by reminding them all have sinned, and encouraging them to confess their sins before God, and to be purified from unrighteousness. He warns to be on guard against the deceiver.

It was Peter and Paul that were sent to the Gentiles to teach them that the kingdom of God was available to them. Recognize the Lord sent these men, it was not something they chose on their own. They were powerful leaders in the Jewish community as well, but they had a unique call from the Holy Spirit to teach the Gentiles.

It should be the desire of every anointed prophet of God honored enough to mentor and teach someone how to operate in the office of a prophet to see their student surpass them in the power and might of the Holy Spirit and in their walk with the Lord.

Questions for Study and Discussion

1. How does one who has been anointed and commissioned to operate in the office of a prophet of God learn how to minister in this office?

2. What is the role of a mentor in the life of a new prophet of God? Who was mentored by Moses?

3. After 40 days in the Lord's presence, how did Moses respond when he came down off the mountain and saw the golden calf?

4. The first time Samuel heard the voice of the Lord, God spoke to him a word of revelation about whom?

5. When Samuel told Eli of the revelation the Lord had given him, what was Eli's response?

6. When the Lord speaks a word to one of His prophets, what is the prophet's obligation?

7. God had Samuel anoint and commission who to be prophets and kings of Israel?

8. Why did God have Samuel anoint David as king of Israel in place of King Saul?

9. How did David view the anointing of the Lord?

10. When Elijah anointed and commissioned Elisha to be a prophet of God, how did Elijah mentor him?

11. Who was more powerful Elijah or Elisha? Explain.

12. Who mentored the disciples? How did He do this?

13. Who mentored the churches after the death of Jesus?

14. Paul and Barnabas had a disagreement concerning what helpers? Explain.

15. Two of the disciples were called by the Lord to take the salvation message to the Gentiles as well as the Jews. Who were they?

16. James, the brother of Jesus, became a leader in what church communities?

17. What should be the desire of every prophet of God when it comes to mentoring?

CHAPTER 24

CLOSING

As I draw this study to a close, I want to encourage everyone to study the scriptures for themselves. Use several translations of the Bible so you can get the full understanding. This will give you the opportunity for the Spirit of God to teach you individually. Read about the prophets of God and how the Holy Spirit operated through each one of them.

I'm sure there are aspects of being a prophet that are not included in this study. I challenge you to learn all you can about the way the prophets represented the Lord on this earth. I also encourage you to ask the Lord to send someone who can mentor you if you have been called and anointed to be a prophet of God.

I do have a caution with regard to being mentored. When you are seeking a mentor let God place that person in your life. Do not attach yourself to anyone without consulting the Lord. Mentoring does not mean that you need to answer to your mentor for all the Lord has you doing. Your true mentor is God Himself and His Holy Spirit.

Let me explain. As a young inexperienced prophet, I agreed that a church counselor would review any word the Lord gave me for the body of Christ, in essence making her my mentor. Now, this counselor was not a prophet, she was simply in authority at the church I was attending. This was not the Lord's direction, and it was a bad idea that became very apparent shortly after making this arrangement.

There came a Sunday when the Lord gave me a word for the body, but this counselor was not in attendance. I prayed and talked with the Lord. He told me He had given me a word, and I was to speak it. I was obedient to the Lord, and gave the message. The next Sunday, the counselor was waiting for me. She began to scold me for speaking a word without her approval. I asked her if she would have me disobey the Lord's assignment in preference to allowing her to review the word before it was spoken. I told her I had to be obedient to the Lord first, and I also told her if ever again she was absent from the service, and the Lord gave me a word, I would do the same thing.

The obligation of the prophet is to obey the Lord first. The Lord will provide someone who is a prophet to mentor you, not just a leader. Your mentor will have years of experience operating as a prophet. Now godly people can mentor other believers, but for a prophet, the mentor needs to be a more experienced prophet.

Understand and remember no one is perfect, even when the Lord sends a mentor your way, don't just copy what they are doing or saying. Take what is good and implement it. Let go of those things that do not resonate with you in the Spirit, and seek the Lord's counsel on this. The Lord will be faithful to show you what is correct and true. He will also show you if what your mentor is doing is wrong. When this happens, tell your mentor what the Lord has shown you, but only after considerable prayer. He will give you direction and the tone with which to address this matter.

It is vital for you to recognize that you are under the authority of the leader in charge of the service when you minister in the church. The pastor or leader of a service is to direct all aspects of the service. This prevents confusion in the service. If the pastor does not allow a word to be given, and it is a word the Lord has directed, the Lord will hold the pastor responsible, not the prophet.

The Lord will also teach you Himself as you seek Him in all you do. Take time to be in the awareness of His presence frequently, and cherish those times of closeness with the Lord. It will strengthen you in your walk with the Lord, and in your ministry as He leads you into the office to which you have been anointed and appointed to serve.

Remember the Lord may teach you through others, but He will teach you directly as well. What you learn directly from the Lord and your mentor will always be backed by scripture.

I have known people who were anointed to be prophets but as they have ministered over time, they have become prideful. They take the credit and honor that is reserved for God alone. By doing this they dishonor their office and the Lord who appointed them. It is crucial for prophets to stay close to the Holy Spirit and seek Him in all they do.

The power that operates through the prophet in the things he says and does is from the Lord God Almighty. When you lose sight of this fact and take the credit for yourself, your anointing will lift allowing you to fall flat on your face. Praise God, when an anointed prophet speaks under the direction of the Holy Spirit, the Lord will stand with him. He defends His prophets when they honor Him.

I am careful to declare if the Lord does not give life to the words I speak in His name, nothing can be accomplished. I acknowledge the words coming from my mouth are His words and not my own. I am simply the vessel through which He speaks.

When I review the words the Lord has spoken through me, I also learn from them. As I give messages the Spirit of God ministers to me as well. I know very well my educational limitations. I know the limitations of my own mind and heart. The words that the Lord speaks through me are far above anything I could come up with on my own.

Being a prophet of God requires flexibility in service to Him. Always check yourself before stepping out in faith. When the Lord sends you out, His anointing will be strong upon you as His messenger.

There is an unscriptural practice observed by many of the Lord's anointed prophets today. This practice is not acknowledging or admitting the Lord has called them to serve in the office of the prophet. It is thought that to do so would be elevating themselves. This unwritten rule indicates it is prideful to admit they have been chosen and anointed by the Holy Spirit to serve in this capacity. I disagree with this practice. There is nothing prideful in admitting you have been called and anointed to serve in this office.

Understand that if someone makes this claim, and they have not, in fact, been commissioned by the Lord to serve; it will quickly become apparent. Nothing in the Word of God suggests that someone is filled with pride because they speak the truth.

Not admitting someone has been appointed to serve in this office is a type of false humility. If you have been chosen by God to serve, be willing to stand in the office and admit it to the body of Christ. It is not prideful to do so. Remember no one who is filled with pride can truly be God's voice to His people. God will humble a person before He places him in the office of the prophet. Do not mistake boldness for pride.

Now, I do admit many prophets can be recognized by the way they operate through the Holy Spirit. One must keep in mind even though someone appears to be a prophet, the Lord calls and anoints His prophets. Unless that call and anointing has been received, one cannot minister in the office of a prophet. Prophets often receive revelation that they speak to the body of Christ, and the fact they are often prophesying in the church makes them very recognizable. There are many who can and do minister through the manifestation gifts of the Holy Spirit. Doing so does not make them prophets, but they are still doing God's work.

Remember also one who ministers in the office of the prophet cannot be a busybody, a manipulator, or a gossip. Participating in these sinful practices will cause a prophet to lack creditability, and it does a disservice to God.

One who lives a life of unrighteousness cannot effectively operate in the office of the prophet even if the Lord has called him to minister in this office. Prophets must be ready to call out sin, and in doing so, their lives must demonstrate pure clean living.

One last thing I need to say. I want to encourage each prophet of God to remain teachable before the Holy Spirit and other prophets. God sends correction to His anointed prophets when they get sidetracked or when they sin. Don't get your feelings hurt and walk away from the Lord and the office to which He has called you. When correction comes do not reject it. Hear what is being said and receive it graciously. Take any correction you receive to the Lord, and if you need to do so, repent.

Scripture says, "My son, do not make light of the Lord's discipline, and do not lose heart when He rebukes you, because the Lord disciplines the one He loves, and He chastens everyone He accepts as His son." (Hebrews 12:5) Usually when a prophet needs to be disciplined, it will be through other prophets who understand how the Holy Spirit operates. The very reason for this is so you can be corrected in love by others who know what it is to hear from the Lord.

Prophets should always be learning through the Holy Spirit. Be open for the Lord to teach you truth from scripture. Allow yourself to be open for Him to give you new insights into old teachings you have known for years.

"The spirits of prophets are subject to the control of prophets." (I Corinthians 14:32) This scripture means that the words prophets speak don't just tumble out of their mouths uncontrolled. Prophets will be taught by the Holy Spirit when to speak once a word is received. Pray over the word until the time the Lord impresses upon you to speak that word. Many who are new in the operation of the manifestation gift of prophecy think it is required that a word be spoken immediately upon receiving it. Sometimes this is true, but more often a word received can be for another time. Through prayer and meditation, the timing of the message will become clear to the prophet.

Be sensitive when you experience a check in your spirit because this will often prevent you from sin or error. This check will also make you aware of false teaching. Allow Him to redirect your path or to give you new direction. You are God's mouthpiece, and your life is an example to the body of Christ. He has assignments for your life you may not yet know; He will direct you as you give Him the opportunity.

Be mindful of the power of the spoken word. Jesus cursed the fig tree when scripture clearly stated, "It was not the season for figs." (Mark 11:13) He did this to display the power of the spoken word, the fig tree withered and died. Remember God Himself spoke the world into being.

James warns us about our tongues saying, "The tongue also is a fire, a world of evil among the parts of the body. It corrupts the whole body, sets the whole course of one's life on fire, and is itself set on fire by hell." (James 3:6) A prophet must be careful not to speak out of anger, hate, or judgment. Always keep in mind the scripture, "If I speak in the tongues of men or of angels, but do not have love, I am only a resounding gong or a clanging cymbal. If I have the gift of prophecy and can fathom all mysteries and all knowledge, and if I have a faith that can move mountains, but do not have love, I am nothing." (I Corinthians 13:1-2)

Whether you have been called to minister in one of the five-fold ministry offices, or if you minister through the manifestation gifts of the Holy Spirit, I encourage you to go forth in the Lord. Allow Him to speak and direct all you do.

Enjoy the journey!

Questions for Study and Discussion

1. Why is it essential for every prophet of God to study the scriptures for themselves?

2. Can just any godly man or woman mentor someone who stands in the office of the prophet?

3. Does God ever have a prophet who is being mentored by another prophet correct the mentor? Explain.

4. The prophet's primary authority is the Lord God Almighty. When operating as a prophet in a public service, who else has authority over the prophet?

5. Who gives the prophet of God power and authority to minister in the office of the prophet?

6. Is it a sign of humility for a prophet to not acknowledge that he is a prophet? Explain.

7. To whom has God given the authority to correct a prophet of God?

8. What is the most essential thing to remember when ministering through the manifestation gifts of the Holy Spirit or as a prophet of God?

RESEARCH MATERIALS

The Holy Spirit and His Gifts, Kenneth E. Hagin, 1980

The Holy Spirit and You, Dennis & Rita Bennett, 1971

The Five-Fold Ministry Offices, Paula A. Price, Ph.D.

Prophecy, Bruce Yocum, 1976

The Prophetic Ministry, Rick Joyner, 1977

The Prophet's Manual, John Eckhardt, 2017

New International Version of the Bible.

BibleHub.com

www.ingramcontent.com/pod-product-compliance
Lightning Source LLC
Chambersburg PA
CBHW021141130626
46554CB00005B/1617